EDITOR: Maryanne Blacker

FOOD EDITOR: Pamela Clark

• • •

ART DIRECTOR: Sue de Guingand

DESIGNERS: Louise Fay, Annemarlene Hissink

• • •

ASSISTANT FOOD EDITORS: Kathy McGarry, Louise Patniotis

ASSOCIATE FOOD EDITOR: Enid Morrison

SENIOR HOME ECONOMIST: Sophia Young

HOME ECONOMISTS: Janene Brooks, Justin Kerr, Caroline Merrillees, Maria Sampsonis, Jodie Tilse, Amal Webster, Lovoni Welch

EDITORIAL COORDINATOR: Elizabeth Hooper

KITCHEN ASSISTANT: Amy Wong

• • •

STYLISTS: Marie-Helene Clauzon, Carolyn Fienberg, Jane Hann, Jacqui Hing, Cherise Koch

PHOTOGRAPHERS: Robert Clark, Robert Taylor

• • •

HOME LIBRARY STAFF:

ASSISTANT EDITORS:
Mary-Anne Danaher, Lynne Testoni

EDITORIAL COORDINATOR: Fiona Lambrou

• • •

ACP CIRCULATION & MARKETING DIRECTOR:
Chris Gibson

CHIEF EXECUTIVE OFFICER: Richard Walsh

PUBLISHER/MANAGING DIRECTOR: Colin Morrison

• • •

Produced by The Australian Women's Weekly Home Library.
Cover separations by ACP Colour Graphics Pty Ltd., Sydney.
Colour separations by Network Graphics Pty. Ltd., Sydney.
Printing by Hannanprint, Sydney.
Published by ACP Publishing Pty. Limited,
54 Park Street, Sydney.
◆ AUSTRALIA: Distributed by Network Distribution
Company, 54 Park Street Sydney, (02) 282 8777.
◆ UNITED KINGDOM: Distributed in the U.K. by Australian
Consolidated Press (UK) Ltd, 20 Galowhill Rd, Brackmills,
Northampton NN4 7EE (01604) 760 456.
◆ CANADA: Distributed in Canada by Whitecap Books Ltd,
351 Lynn Ave, North Vancouver B.C. V7J 2C4 (604) 980 9852.
◆ NEW ZEALAND: Distributed in New Zealand by Netlink
Distribution Company, 17B Hargreaves St, Level 5,
College Hill, Auckland 1 (9) 302 7616.
◆ SOUTH AFRICA: Distributed in South Africa by Intermag,
PO Box 57394, Springfield 2137, Johannesburg (011) 491 7534.

• • •

Muffins, Scones & Breads

Includes index.
ISBN 1 86396 049 X

1. Cookery (Bread) 2. Scones. 3. Muffins.
(Series: Australian Women's Weekly
Home Library).

641.815

• • •

© A C P Publishing Pty. Limited 1996
ACN 053 273 546
◆ This publication is copyright. No part of it may
be reproduced or transmitted in any form without the
written permission of the publishers.

• • •

COVER: Clockwise from top: Turkish Bread, page 60;
Peppery Lots-of-Seed Scones, page 119; Pagnotta, page 67;
Prosciutto, Basil and Tomato Muffins, page 30.
OPPOSITE: Fig and Apple Turnover, page 105.
BACK COVER: Passionfruit, Pineapple and
Mint Muffins, page 32.

*We would like to thank Doreen Badger, Bread Institute
of Australia, for her assistance.*

Muffins, Scones & Breads

The aroma of freshly baked bread and scones is one of life's pleasures, and a muffin laced with chocolate or fruit is pure temptation. Forget any tales about bread-making being best practised by those with a lot of patience and time, because our step-by-step techniques and helpful tips will ensure that, in no time at all, you'll feel confident making even the most exotic breads! Our practical advice also takes the mystery out of scone- and muffin-making so that the lightest of scones and the most luscious muffins will be easy to bake.

Pamela Clark

FOOD EDITOR

BRITISH & NORTH AMERICAN READERS: Please note that
Australian cup and spoon measurements are metric. A quick conversion
guide appears on page 127.
A glossary explaining unfamiliar terms and ingredients appears on page 122.

Muffins

Muffins are simple to make and delicious eaten hot, warm or cold, and with or without butter. They are best made on the day of serving. All of our recipes will make either 12 medium or 6 large muffins.

■ We used a medium-sized muffin pan (1/3 cup/80ml capacity), and a larger, Texas-style muffin pan (3/4 cup/180ml capacity). Other sized pans are available, but you will need to adjust baking times if you use these pans. Pans should be slightly more than half-filled with mixture, whatever size pans you use. Pans should be greased evenly or coated with a non-stick spray.

■ Butter should be firm from the refrigerator when it is to be chopped.

■ Muffin mixtures require minimum mixing and should look coarse and lumpy. We found a large metal spoon or fork the best implement for mixing.

■ To test if muffins are cooked – they should be browned, risen, firm to touch and beginning to shrink from sides of pan. If in doubt, push a metal or wooden skewer into a muffin. When withdrawn, the skewer should be clean and free from muffin mixture. Turn muffins from the pan onto a wire rack as soon as they are baked to prevent them becoming steamy. However, if muffins have a filling such as custard, caramel or jam, let them stand a few minutes before turning them onto a wire rack. These fillings can be extremely hot, so handle them carefully.

■ Cold muffins freeze well; transfer to freezer wrap or freezer bags before freezing. Press bag gently or use a freezer pump to expel all the air. Correctly wrapped muffins can be frozen for up to 3 months.

■ To thaw in a conventional oven, remove freezer wrap and re-wrap muffins individually in foil, place in a single layer on an oven tray in a moderate oven for about 20 minutes or until they reach the right eating temperature for you.

■ Microwave ovens vary in power, so we can give only a general guide to thawing muffins this way. Remove freezer wrap from muffins, place in a single layer in the oven. Set the oven on **DEFROST, MEDIUM LOW or 30%**, according to your oven. Allow about 45 seconds for 1 muffin; 1 minute for 2 muffins; and 1 1/2 minutes for 4 muffins. Stand muffins for 10 to 15 seconds. Thawed muffins should not feel hot to the touch. If they feel hot, they are overheated. You may need to experiment for best results.

■ These recipes have not been tested to cook in a microwave oven.

First tier: Basic Muffins; Choc Chip and Walnut. Second tier: Date and Orange; Fruit and Spice.

Tiered stand from Le Forge

BASIC MUFFINS

2½ cups (375g) self-raising flour
90g butter, chopped
1 cup (220g) caster sugar
1¼ cups (310ml) buttermilk
1 egg, lightly beaten

1. Grease 12 hole (⅓ cup/80ml capacity) muffin pan. Sift flour into large bowl, rub in butter.

2. Stir in sugar, buttermilk and egg. Do not over-mix; batter should be lumpy.

3. Spoon mixture into prepared pan. Bake in moderately hot oven about 20 minutes.

Makes 12.

VARIATIONS

FRUIT AND SPICE

3 teaspoons mixed spice
1 cup (190g) mixed dried fruit

Sift spice with flour; add fruit with sugar.

DATE AND ORANGE

1 cup (160g) wholemeal
  self-raising flour
1½ cups (240g) seeded
  chopped dates
3 teaspoons grated orange rind

Substitute 1 cup of the self-raising flour in basic muffin recipe with the wholemeal self-raising flour. Add dates and rind with sugar.

CHOC CHIP AND WALNUT

¾ cup (140g) Choc Bits
1 cup (120g) chopped walnuts

Add Choc Bits and nuts with sugar.

CHOCOLATE BEETROOT MUFFINS

2 large (500g) beetroot
1³/4 cups (260g) self-raising flour
¹/3 cup (35g) cocoa powder
1 cup (220g) caster sugar
2 eggs, lightly beaten
¹/3 cup (80ml) vegetable oil
¹/3 cup (80ml) buttermilk

Grease 12 hole (¹/3 cup/80ml capacity) muffin pan.

Wash and trim beetroot, cut off leaves, leaving about 3cm stem attached. Boil, steam or microwave unpeeled beetroot until tender. Drain beetroot, rinse under cold water, drain. Peel beetroot while warm, blend or process until smooth. You need 1¹/3 cups (330ml) beetroot puree.

Sift dry ingredients into large bowl, stir in beetroot and remaining ingredients. Spoon into prepared pan. Bake in moderately hot oven about 25 minutes.

Makes 12.

PASSIONFRUIT-GLAZED BERRY MUFFINS

We used a combination of fresh strawberries and frozen boysenberries in this recipe.

2¹/2 cups (375g) self-raising flour
³/4 cup (165g) caster sugar
1 egg, lightly beaten
60g butter, melted
1¹/4 cups (310ml) buttermilk
1¹/3 cups (200g) mixed fresh or frozen berries

PASSIONFRUIT GLAZE
2 passionfruit
1 tablespoon caster sugar
1 teaspoon gelatine

Grease 12 hole (¹/3 cup/80ml capacity) muffin pan.

Sift flour and sugar into large bowl, stir in egg, butter and buttermilk, then berries. Spoon mixture into prepared pan. Bake in moderately hot oven about 20 minutes. Brush hot muffins with hot passionfruit glaze.

Passionfruit Glaze: Remove pulp from passionfruit, strain, discard seeds. You will need 2 tablespoons of passionfruit juice. Combine juice with sugar and gelatine in small pan, stir over heat, without boiling, until gelatine is dissolved.

Makes 12.

ABOVE: Passionfruit-Glazed Berry Muffins.
RIGHT: Chocolate Beetroot Muffins.

CRANBERRY CAMEMBERT MUFFINS

2 cups (300g) self-raising flour
2 tablespoons caster sugar
2 eggs, lightly beaten
1/3 cup (80ml) cranberry sauce
**125g camembert cheese,
     finely chopped**
1/2 cup (125ml) plain yogurt
1/4 cup (60ml) milk
60g butter, melted
**1/2 cup (125ml) cranberry
     sauce, extra**
1/3 cup (40g) chopped walnuts

Grease 12 hole (1/3 cup/80ml capacity) muffin pan.

Sift dry ingredients into large bowl, stir in eggs, sauce, cheese, yogurt, milk and butter. Half-fill prepared pan with mixture, make a well in each muffin, drop rounded teaspoons of extra sauce into each well, top with remaining muffin mixture. Sprinkle with nuts. Bake in moderately hot oven about 20 minutes. Makes 12.

BANANA MAPLE MUFFINS

*You will need about 2 small (280g)
over-ripe bananas for this recipe.*

2 cups (300g) self-raising flour
1/3 cup (50g) plain flour
1/2 teaspoon bicarbonate of soda
**1/2 cup (100g) firmly packed
     brown sugar**
1/4 cup (60ml) maple-flavoured syrup
2/3 cup mashed bananas
2 eggs, lightly beaten
1 cup (250ml) buttermilk
1/3 cup (80ml) vegetable oil

COCONUT TOPPING
15g butter
1 tablespoon maple-flavoured syrup
2/3 cup (30g) flaked coconut

Grease 12 hole (1/3 cup/80ml capacity) muffin pan.

Sift dry ingredients into large bowl. Stir in maple syrup and bananas, then eggs, buttermilk and oil. Spoon mixture into prepared pan, sprinkle with coconut topping. Bake in moderately hot oven about 20 minutes.
Coconut Topping: Melt butter in small pan, add maple syrup and coconut, stir constantly over heat until coconut is lightly browned.
Makes 12.

*LEFT: Cranberry Camembert Muffins.
ABOVE RIGHT: Banana Maple Muffins.
RIGHT: Chocolate Hazelnut Muffins.*

Knife and wire basket from The Bay Tree Kitchen Shop, plate from Accoutrement

CHOCOLATE HAZELNUT MUFFINS

2¹/₂ cups (375g) self-raising flour
¹/₂ teaspoon bicarbonate of soda
¹/₄ cup (25g) cocoa powder
¹/₂ cup (100g) firmly packed
   brown sugar
125g butter, melted
2 eggs, lightly beaten
1 cup (250ml) buttermilk
1 cup (250ml) Nutella

Grease 12 hole (¹/₃ cup/80ml capacity) muffin pan.

Sift dry ingredients into large bowl, stir in butter, eggs and buttermilk. Spoon one-third of the mixture into prepared pan, top with 1 tablespoon of Nutella. Top with remaining muffin mixture. Bake in moderately hot oven about 20 minutes.
Makes 12.

CURRIED CHICKEN MUFFINS

1 tablespoon vegetable oil
1 small (80g) onion, finely chopped
3 (330g) chicken thigh fillets,
  finely chopped
2 tablespoons Madras curry paste
1 cup (250ml) plain yogurt
2¼ cups (335g) self-raising flour
½ cup (125ml) vegetable oil, extra
2 eggs, lightly beaten
2 tablespoons lemon juice
2 tablespoons chopped fresh
  coriander leaves
ground hot paprika

Grease 12 hole (⅓ cup/80ml capacity) muffin pan.

Heat oil in pan, add onion, stir over heat until onion is soft. Add chicken, stir over heat until chicken is just tender, stir in curry paste, remove from heat, stir in yogurt; cool.

Sift flour into large bowl, stir in chicken mixture, extra oil, eggs, juice and coriander. Spoon mixture into prepared pan, sprinkle with a little paprika. Bake in moderately hot oven about 20 minutes.

Makes 12.

LEFT: Curried Chicken Muffins.
RIGHT: Chick Pea and Spinach Muffins.
BELOW: Spicy Sausage and Corn Muffins.

SPICY SAUSAGE AND CORN MUFFINS

1¾ cups (260g) self-raising flour
1 teaspoon dried crushed chillies
½ teaspoon ground cumin
½ teaspoon ground coriander
1 teaspoon ground hot paprika
¾ cup (90g) coarsely grated
  smoked cheese
90g chorizo sausage, chopped
½ medium (100g) red
  pepper, chopped
½ medium (100g) green
  pepper, chopped
1 clove garlic, crushed
1 small (80g) onion, grated
130g can creamed corn
2 eggs, lightly beaten
90g butter, melted
1 cup (250ml) buttermilk
½ teaspoon ground hot paprika, extra

Grease 6 hole (¾ cup/180ml capacity) muffin pan.

Sift flour into large bowl, add chillies, spices, cheese, sausage and peppers; mix well. Add garlic, onion and corn, then stir in eggs, butter and buttermilk. Spoon mixture into prepared pan, sprinkle with extra paprika. Bake in moderately hot oven about 25 minutes.

Makes 6.

CHICK PEA AND SPINACH MUFFINS

1/4 cup (40g) cornmeal
1 tablespoon vegetable oil
4 green shallots, chopped
2 cloves garlic, crushed
40 leaves English
  spinach, shredded
2 cups (300g) self-raising flour
1 cup (170g) cornmeal, extra
2 tablespoons finely chopped
  fresh basil
1 egg, lightly beaten
1 1/4 cups (310ml) milk
90g butter, melted
300g can chick peas,
  rinsed, drained
2 tablespoons finely grated
  parmesan cheese

Grease 6 hole (3/4 cup/180ml capacity) muffin pan.

Sprinkle inside of pans with about half the cornmeal. Heat oil in medium pan, add shallots and garlic, cook, stirring, until shallots are just soft. Add spinach, cook, stirring, until spinach is just wilted; cool.

Sift flour and extra cornmeal into large bowl, stir in basil, egg, milk and butter, then spinach mixture and chick peas. Spoon mixture into prepared pan, sprinkle with cheese and remaining cornmeal. Bake in moderately hot oven about 25 minutes.

Makes 6.

LEMON RASPBERRY MUFFINS

2 cups (300g) self-raising flour
2 teaspoons grated lemon rind
1/3 cup (75g) caster sugar
1 egg, lightly beaten
60g butter, melted
1 cup (250ml) buttermilk
200g frozen raspberries

LEMON GLAZE
1 tablespoon lemon juice
1 teaspoon gelatine
1½ tablespoons caster sugar

Grease 6 hole (3/4 cup/180ml capacity) muffin pan.

Sift flour into large bowl, stir in rind and sugar, then egg, butter and buttermilk, then raspberries. Spoon mixture into prepared pan. Bake in moderately hot oven about 25 minutes. Brush with hot glaze while muffins are hot.
Lemon Glaze: Combine all ingredients in small pan, stir over heat, without boiling, until gelatine is dissolved.
Makes 6.

NUTTY PEAR MUFFINS

2½ cups (375g) self-raising flour
1 cup (125g) chopped pecans
1 teaspoon cracked black pepper
150g soft blue cheese, chopped
425g can pear halves in light syrup,
**   drained, chopped**
2 eggs, lightly beaten
½ cup (125ml) vegetable oil
½ cup (125ml) milk

Grease 12 hole (⅓ cup/80ml capacity) muffin pan.

Sift flour into large bowl, stir in nuts, pepper, cheese and pears, then eggs, oil and milk. Spoon mixture into prepared pan, sprinkle with a little extra cracked pepper. Bake in moderately hot oven about 20 minutes.

Makes 12.

CHOCOLATE ORANGE DESSERT MUFFINS

2 cups (300g) self-raising flour
½ cup (50g) cocoa powder
1¼ cups (275g) caster sugar
125g butter, melted
¾ cup (180ml) buttermilk
1 egg, lightly beaten
2 tablespoons Grand Marnier
2 teaspoons grated orange rind
12 (120g) chocolate orange thins

CREME ANGLAISE
4 egg yolks
½ cup (110g) caster sugar
1⅔ cups (410ml) milk

Grease 12 hole (⅓ cup/80ml capacity) muffin pan.

Sift flour, cocoa and sugar into large bowl, stir in butter, buttermilk, egg, liqueur and rind. Spoon mixture into prepared pan. Break each chocolate into 3 or 4 pieces, push chocolate into each muffin. Make sure that chocolate does not touch sides of muffin pan and that mixture almost covers the chocolate. Bake in moderately hot oven about 20 minutes. Serve muffins with creme anglaise.

Creme Anglaise: Beat egg yolks and sugar in small bowl with electric mixer until thick and pale. Place milk in pan, bring to the boil, whisk milk into yolk mixture. Return mixture to pan, stir over heat, without boiling, until mixture thickens and coats back of spoon.

Makes 12.

BELOW: Chocolate Orange Dessert Muffins.
BELOW LEFT: Lemon Raspberry Muffins.
LEFT: Nutty Pear Muffins.

Setting from Dinosaur Designs

WHITE CHOCOLATE AND MACADAMIA MUFFINS

2 cups (300g) self-raising flour
2/3 cup (150g) caster sugar
3/4 cup (140g) White Bits
1/2 cup (75g) chopped macadamias, toasted
60g butter, melted
3/4 cup (180ml) milk
1 egg, lightly beaten

Grease 6 hole (3/4 cup/180ml capacity) muffin pan.

Sift dry ingredients into large bowl, stir in remaining ingredients. Spoon mixture into prepared pan. Bake in moderately hot oven about 25 minutes.
Makes 6.

GINGER DATE MUFFINS WITH CARAMEL SAUCE

1 cup (160g) seeded chopped dates
1/3 cup (80ml) water
1/4 teaspoon bicarbonate of soda
2 cups (300g) self-raising flour
1 cup (150g) plain flour
2 teaspoons ground ginger
1/2 teaspoon mixed spice
1 cup (200g) firmly packed brown sugar
2 teaspoons grated orange rind
1 egg, lightly beaten
1 1/4 cups (310ml) milk
1/4 cup (60ml) vegetable oil

CARAMEL SAUCE
1 cup (200g) firmly packed brown sugar
1 cup (250ml) cream
40g butter

Grease 12 hole (1/3 cup/80ml capacity) muffin pan.

Combine dates and water in pan, bring to boil, remove from heat, add soda, stand 5 minutes. Sift dry ingredients into large bowl, stir in date mixture and remaining ingredients. Spoon mixture into prepared pan. Bake in moderately hot oven about 20 minutes. Serve warm muffins with caramel sauce.
Caramel Sauce: Combine all ingredients in pan, stir over heat, without boiling, until sugar is dissolved, then simmer, without stirring, 3 minutes.

Makes 12.

ABOVE: White Chocolate and Macadamia Muffins.
RIGHT: Ginger Date Muffins with Caramel Sauce.

CRUSTY ONION AND CHEESE MUFFINS

1/4 cup (35g) plain flour
20g butter
1 teaspoon water, approximately
1 tablespoon vegetable oil
1 medium (150g) onion,
  halved, sliced
1 3/4 cups (260g) self-raising flour
3/4 cup (110g) plain flour, extra
3/4 cup (90g) grated tasty
  cheddar cheese
1 tablespoon chopped fresh chives
1 egg, lightly beaten
1 1/4 cups (310ml) buttermilk
1/2 cup (125ml) vegetable oil, extra

CHIVE BUTTER
50g packaged cream cheese,
  softened
50g butter, softened
2 teaspoons lemon juice
1 tablespoon chopped fresh chives

Place plain flour into small bowl, rub in butter, mix in just enough water to bind ingredients. Press dough into a ball, cover, freeze about 30 minutes or until firm. Grease 6 hole (3/4 cup/180ml capacity) muffin pan. Heat oil in frying pan, add onion, cook, stirring, until soft and lightly browned; cool.

Sift self-raising and extra plain flour into large bowl, stir in half the onion, half the cheese and all the chives, then egg, buttermilk and extra oil. Spoon mixture into prepared pan. Coarsely grate frozen dough into small bowl, quickly mix in remaining onion and cheese; sprinkle over muffins. Bake in moderately hot oven about 25 minutes. Serve with chive butter.

Chive Butter: Beat cheese and butter together in small bowl until smooth, stir in juice and chives.

Makes 6.

SMOKED CHEESE AND SALAMI MUFFINS

2 cups (300g) self-raising flour
1 cup (150g) plain flour
90g butter, melted
1 egg, lightly beaten
1 1/2 cups (375ml) buttermilk
12 slices (140g) mild salami,
  finely chopped
140g smoked cheese,
  finely chopped
1 tablespoon chopped fresh parsley
2 teaspoons chopped fresh thyme
1 teaspoon seasoned pepper

Grease 12 hole (1/3 cup/80ml capacity) muffin pan.

Sift flours into large bowl, stir in remaining ingredients. Spoon mixture into prepared pan. Bake in moderately hot oven about 20 minutes.

Makes 12.

CHEESY PIZZA MUFFINS

1 small (150g) red pepper
2½ cups (375g) self-raising flour
1 egg, lightly beaten
1¼ cups (310ml) milk
⅓ cup (80ml) light olive oil
½ cup (60g) grated tasty
   cheddar cheese
¼ cup (20g) grated fresh
   parmesan cheese
½ cup (60g) seeded black
   olives, halved
¼ cup (35g) drained chopped
   sun-dried tomatoes
2 tablespoons chopped fresh basil
2 teaspoons chopped fresh
   rosemary
¼ cup (30g) grated tasty cheddar
   cheese, extra

Grease 6 hole (¾ cup/180ml capacity) muffin pan.

Quarter pepper, remove seeds and membranes. Grill pepper, skin side up, until skin blisters and blackens. Peel away skin, cut pepper into strips.

Sift flour into large bowl, stir in egg, milk, oil, cheeses, olives, tomatoes and herbs. Spoon mixture into prepared pan, top with pepper strips, sprinkle with extra cheese. Bake in moderately hot oven about 25 minutes.

Makes 6.

LEFT: Cheesy Pizza Muffins.
BELOW: Smoked Cheese and Salami Muffins.
FAR LEFT: Crusty Onion and Cheese Muffins.

Setting from Storehouse

Stainless steel tray from Ventura Design

CINNAMON PEAR MUFFINS

**425g can pear halves in
  natural juice**
2½ cups (375g) self-raising flour
½ teaspoon ground cinnamon
**⅔ cup (130g) firmly packed
  brown sugar**
**½ cup (60g) packaged ground
  almonds**
90g butter, melted
1 egg, lightly beaten
⅔ cup (160ml) cream
extra ground cinnamon

Grease 12 hole (⅓ cup/80ml capacity) muffin pan.

Drain pears, reserve ½ cup (125ml) of juice. Place pears on absorbent paper, pat dry. Chop pears finely.

Sift dry ingredients into large bowl, stir in pears, reserved juice, nuts, butter, egg and cream. Spoon mixture into prepared pan, sprinkle with a little extra cinnamon. Bake in moderately hot oven about 20 minutes.

Makes 12.

CUSTARD SURPRISE MUFFINS

1⅔ cups (250g) self-raising flour
1 cup (150g) plain flour
**¾ cup (150g) firmly packed
  brown sugar**
2 tablespoons custard powder
½ teaspoon ground cinnamon
¼ teaspoon ground cloves
1 cup (250ml) milk
½ cup (125ml) vegetable oil
20g butter, melted
2 eggs, lightly beaten
1 teaspoon ground cinnamon, extra
2 tablespoons caster sugar

CUSTARD FILLING
1 tablespoon custard powder
2 tablespoons caster sugar
½ cup (125ml) milk
1 teaspoon vanilla essence

Grease 6 hole (¾ cup/180ml capacity) muffin pan.

Sift flours, brown sugar, custard powder and spices into large bowl, stir in milk, oil, butter and eggs. Spoon half the mixture into prepared pan, make a well in each muffin, spoon custard into wells. Top with remaining muffin mixture, sprinkle with combined extra cinnamon and caster sugar. Bake muffins in moderately hot oven about 25 minutes.

Custard Filling: Combine custard powder and sugar in small pan, gradually stir in milk, stir over heat until mixture comes to the boil. Stir in essence, cover surface of custard with plastic wrap; cool.

Makes 6.

*RIGHT: Coconut Lemon Syrup Muffins.
BELOW RIGHT: Custard Surprise Muffins.
BELOW: Cinnamon Pear Muffins.*

Setting from House

COCONUT LEMON SYRUP MUFFINS

2 cups (300g) self-raising flour
90g butter
3/4 cup (165g) caster sugar
1 cup (90g) coconut
1 tablespoon grated lemon rind
1 egg, lightly beaten
1 cup (250ml) coconut cream
2 tablespoons shredded coconut

LEMON SYRUP
1/2 cup (110g) caster sugar
1/4 cup (60ml) water
2 teaspoons grated lemon rind
1/4 cup (60ml) lemon juice

Grease 12 hole (1/3 cup/80ml capacity) muffin pan.

Sift flour into large bowl, rub in butter. Stir in sugar, coconut, rind, egg and coconut cream. Spoon mixture into prepared pan, sprinkle with shredded coconut. Bake in moderately hot oven about 20 minutes. Pour hot lemon syrup over hot muffins, then turn onto wire rack to cool.

Lemon Syrup: Combine all ingredients in small pan, stir over heat, without boiling, until sugar is dissolved, then simmer 2 minutes without stirring.

Makes 12.

BANANA DATE MUFFINS

You will need about 2 large (460g) over-ripe bananas for this recipe.

2 cups (300g) self-raising flour
1 teaspoon mixed spice
1/2 cup (100g) firmly packed
   brown sugar
1 cup mashed bananas
1 cup (160g) seeded chopped dates
3 eggs, lightly beaten
1/3 cup (80ml) vegetable oil
1/3 cup (80ml) buttermilk

Grease 12 hole (1/3 cup/80ml capacity) muffin pan.

Sift dry ingredients into large bowl, stir in remaining ingredients. Spoon mixture into prepared pan. Bake in moderately hot oven about 20 minutes. Makes 12.

BLACKBERRY STREUSEL MUFFINS

2 cups (300g) self-raising flour
1 1/4 cups (170g) frozen blackberries
1 medium (150g) apple, peeled,
   coarsely grated
3/4 cup (150g) firmly packed
   brown sugar
3 eggs, lightly beaten
1/3 cup (80ml) vegetable oil
1/3 cup (80ml) buttermilk

STREUSEL TOPPING
1/3 cup (50g) plain flour
2 tablespoons brown sugar
1 teaspoon mixed spice
30g butter

Grease 12 hole (1/3 cup/80ml capacity) muffin pan.

Sift flour into large bowl, stir in remaining ingredients. Spoon mixture into prepared pan. Coarsely grate streusel topping over muffins. Bake in moderately hot oven about 20 minutes.
Streusel Topping: Sift flour, sugar and spice into small bowl; rub in butter. Roll mixture into a ball, wrap in plastic wrap, freeze until firm enough to grate. Makes 12.

APRICOT DATE MUFFINS

You will need about 2 large (460g) over-ripe bananas for this recipe.

1 cup (160g) seeded chopped dates
1/2 cup (75g) chopped dried apricots
100g butter, chopped
2/3 cup (130g) firmly packed brown sugar
1/4 cup (60ml) water
1 1/4 cups (200g) wholemeal self-raising flour
1/2 teaspoon bicarbonate of soda
1 cup mashed bananas
1 cup (35g) Bran Flakes
1 egg, lightly beaten
1/2 cup (15g) Bran Flakes, extra

Grease 12 hole (1/3 cup/80ml capacity) muffin pan.

Combine dates, apricots, butter, sugar and water in pan, stir over heat until butter is melted. Bring to boil, simmer, uncovered, 1 minute; cool.

Sift flour and soda into large bowl, stir in date mixture, bananas, Bran Flakes and egg. Spoon mixture into prepared pan, sprinkle with extra Bran Flakes. Bake in moderately hot oven about 20 minutes.

Makes 12.

BELOW: Blackberry Streusel Muffins.
FAR LEFT: Banana Date Muffins.
LEFT: Apricot Date Muffins.

ROASTED PEPPER AND FETA MUFFINS

1 medium (200g) red pepper
1 medium (200g) yellow pepper
2½ cups (375g) self-raising flour
100g feta cheese, chopped
½ cup (40g) grated fresh
  parmesan cheese
90g butter, melted
1 egg, lightly beaten
1 cup (250ml) milk
1 tablespoon chopped
  fresh rosemary
½ teaspoon ground black pepper
1 tablespoon sesame seeds

Grease 6 hole (3/4 cup/180ml capacity) muffin pan.

Quarter peppers, remove seeds and membranes. Grill peppers, skin side up, until skin blisters and blackens. Peel skin away, roughly chop peppers.

Sift flour into large bowl, stir in red and yellow peppers, cheeses, butter, egg, milk, rosemary and black pepper. Spoon mixture into prepared pan, sprinkle with seeds. Bake in moderately hot oven about 30 minutes. Makes 6.

ARRABIATA MUFFINS

3 (120g) bacon rashers,
  finely chopped
2 cups (300g) self-raising flour
1 cup (150g) plain flour
1/3 cup (25g) coarsely grated fresh
  parmesan cheese
3/4 cup (90g) seeded sliced
  black olives
2 tablespoons shredded fresh basil
1 tablespoon chopped
  fresh oregano
2 eggs, lightly beaten
2 tablespoons tomato puree
3 teaspoons sambal oelek
3 cloves garlic, crushed
3/4 cup (180ml) vegetable oil
1½ cups (375ml) buttermilk
1 tablespoon shredded fresh
  basil, extra

Grease 12 hole (1/3 cup/80ml capacity) muffin pan.

Cook bacon in heated pan until crisp, drain on absorbent paper; cool. Sift flours into large bowl, stir in bacon, cheese, olives and herbs, then eggs, puree, sambal oelek, garlic, oil and buttermilk. Spoon mixture into prepared pan, sprinkle with extra basil. Bake in moderately hot oven about 20 minutes. Makes 12.

THREE CHEESE MUFFINS

2 cups (300g) self-raising flour
½ teaspoon vegetable stock powder
80g butter
3/4 cup (90g) coarsely grated tasty
  cheddar cheese
½ cup (40g) finely grated fresh
  parmesan cheese
1/4 cup (60g) crumbled blue
  vein cheese
1 egg, lightly beaten
1 cup (250ml) milk
2 teaspoons Dijon mustard
2 green shallots, finely chopped

Grease 12 hole (1/3 cup/80ml capacity) muffin pan.

Sift dry ingredients into large bowl, rub in butter. Stir in remaining ingredients. Spoon mixture into prepared pan. Bake in moderately hot oven about 20 minutes.
Makes 12.

ABOVE: Roasted Pepper and Feta Muffins.
TOP: Three Cheese Muffins.
RIGHT: Arrabiata Muffins.

Plate from House

CURRIED SALMON MUFFINS

90g butter
2 teaspoons green curry paste
210g can salmon, drained
2¹/₂ cups (375g) self-raising flour
¹/₄ cup chopped fresh
  coriander leaves
2 teaspoons grated lime rind
1 cup (250ml) coconut milk
²/₃ cup (160ml) buttermilk
2 eggs, lightly beaten
¹/₄ cup (35g) roasted unsalted
  peanuts, finely chopped
1 tablespoon mild sweet chilli sauce
1 teaspoon grated lime rind
1 clove garlic, crushed
1 teaspoon grated fresh ginger

Grease 12 hole (¹/₃ cup/80ml capacity) muffin pan.

Melt butter in medium pan, add curry paste, stir over heat until fragrant, stir in salmon. Sift flour into large bowl, stir in coriander and rind, then salmon mixture, coconut milk, buttermilk and eggs. Spoon mixture into prepared pan, sprinkle with combined remaining ingredients. Bake in moderately hot oven about 20 minutes.
Makes 12.

LEFT: Curried Salmon Muffins.
ABOVE: Caramelised Onion and Polenta Muffins.
RIGHT: Peppered Zucchini and Leek Muffins.

CARAMELISED ONION AND POLENTA MUFFINS

2 tablespoons olive oil
3 medium (450g) onions, sliced
1 teaspoon cumin seeds
1 teaspoon dried crushed chillies
2 tablespoons white vinegar
2 tablespoons caster sugar
3 cups (450g) self-raising flour
2 cups (340g) polenta
2 eggs, lightly beaten
185g butter, melted
1 1/3 cups (330ml) milk
1/4 cup chopped fresh parsley
1 tablespoon chopped fresh thyme

Grease 12 hole (1/3 cup/80ml capacity) muffin pan.

Heat oil in pan, add onions, seeds and chillies, cook, stirring, until onions are soft. Add vinegar and sugar, cook, stirring occasionally, about 20 minutes or until onions are golden brown; cool. Reserve 1/4 cup onion mixture.

Sift flour into large bowl, stir in onion mixture with remaining ingredients. Spoon mixture into prepared pan. Bake in moderately hot oven about 20 minutes. Serve muffins topped with the reserved onion mixture.
Makes 12.

PEPPERED ZUCCHINI AND LEEK MUFFINS

1 tablespoon olive oil
1 medium (350g) leek, sliced
3 small (270g) zucchini, grated
2 cloves garlic, crushed
2 cups (300g) self-raising flour
2 teaspoons curry powder
1 teaspoon ground coriander
1 teaspoon ground cumin
100g butter, chopped
1/2 cup (60g) grated tasty
    cheddar cheese
2 eggs, lightly beaten
1 cup (250ml) buttermilk
2 tablespoons olive oil, extra

TOPPING
3/4 cup (90g) grated tasty
    cheddar cheese
1 teaspoon cracked black pepper
1 teaspoon sea salt

Grease 12 hole (1/3 cup/80ml capacity) muffin pan.

Heat oil in frying pan, add leek, zucchini and garlic, cook, stirring, until leek is soft and any liquid evaporated. Strain mixture, press out excess liquid; cool.

Sift flour, curry powder and spices into large bowl, rub in butter, stir in zucchini mixture and cheese, then eggs, buttermilk and extra oil. Spoon mixture into prepared pan, sprinkle with topping. Bake in moderately hot oven about 20 minutes.
Topping: Combine all ingredients in small bowl; mix well.
Makes 12.

Setting from Orson & Blake Collectables

CITRUS POPPYSEED MUFFINS

125g soft butter
2 teaspoons grated lemon rind
2 teaspoons grated lime rind
2 teaspoons grated orange rind
2/3 cup (150g) caster sugar
2 eggs
2 cups (300g) self-raising flour
1/2 cup (125ml) milk
2 tablespoons poppyseeds

Grease 12 hole (1/3 cup/80ml capacity) muffin pan.

Place butter, rinds, sugar, eggs, sifted flour and milk in medium bowl, beat with electric mixer until just combined, then beat on medium speed until mixture is smooth and just changed in colour; stir in poppyseeds. Spoon mixture into prepared pan. Bake in moderately hot oven about 20 minutes. Makes 12.

CHOC HONEYCOMB MUFFINS

2 cups (300g) self-raising flour
1/4 cup (55g) caster sugar
1 cup (190g) White Bits
100g chocolate-coated
    honeycomb, chopped
1 egg, lightly beaten
60g butter, melted
1 cup (250ml) buttermilk
1/4 cup (60ml) honey
1 teaspoon vanilla essence

Grease 12 hole (1/3 cup/80ml capacity) muffin pan.

Sift flour and sugar into large bowl, stir in White Bits and honeycomb, then remaining ingredients. Spoon mixture into prepared pan. Bake in moderately hot oven about 20 minutes.
Makes 12.

CRUNCHY NUT 'N' MUESLI MUFFINS

1/3 x 250g packet Butternut Cookies
1 1/2 cups (225g) self-raising flour
1/2 cup (75g) plain flour
100g butter, chopped
1/2 cup (65g) toasted muesli
2 eggs, lightly beaten
3/4 cup (180ml) milk
2/3 cup (160ml) canned sweetened
    condensed milk

TOPPING
2 tablespoons chopped walnuts
2 tablespoons slivered almonds
2 tablespoons flaked coconut
1 tablespoon toasted muesli
1 tablespoon brown sugar

Grease 12 hole (1/3 cup/80ml capacity) muffin pan.

Crush or process cookies until fine. Sift flours into large bowl, rub in butter. Stir in crumbs and muesli, then eggs, milk and condensed milk. Spoon mixture into prepared pan, sprinkle with topping. Bake in moderately hot oven about 20 minutes.
Topping: Combine all ingredients in small bowl; mix well.
Makes 12.

Basket from Francalia; tiles from Country Floors

LEFT: Crunchy Nut 'n' Muesli Muffins.
ABOVE LEFT: Citrus Poppyseed Muffins.
RIGHT: Choc Honeycomb Muffins.

BLUEBERRY MUFFINS

2 cups (300g) self-raising flour
3/4 cup (150g) firmly packed
brown sugar
1 cup (150g) fresh or frozen
blueberries
1 egg, lightly beaten
3/4 cup (180ml) buttermilk
1/2 cup (125ml) vegetable oil

Grease 6 hole (3/4 cup/180ml capacity) muffin pan.

Sift dry ingredients into large bowl, stir in remaining ingredients. Spoon mixture into prepared pan. Bake in moderately hot oven about 25 minutes.

Makes 6.

PASSIONFRUIT NUT MUFFINS

2 cups (300g) self-raising flour
1 teaspoon mixed spice
80g butter
1 cup (110g) packaged
ground hazelnuts
1 cup (220g) caster sugar
1 egg, lightly beaten
3/4 cup (180ml) milk

FILLING
170g can passionfruit in syrup
1½ tablespoons caster sugar
2 tablespoons water
1 tablespoon cornflour

Grease 6 hole (3/4 cup/180ml capacity) muffin pan.

Sift flour and spice into large bowl, rub in butter. Stir in nuts and sugar, then egg and milk. Spoon mixture into prepared pan. Using a spatula, make a well in each muffin, spoon filling into wells. Bake in moderately hot oven about 25 minutes.

Filling: Combine passionfruit and sugar in small pan, stir in blended water and cornflour, stir over heat until mixture boils and thickens; cool 5 minutes.

Makes 6.

ABOVE: Blueberry Muffins.
RIGHT: Passionfruit Nut Muffins.

Wooden bowls from Cornucopia Gallery

CHOC CHIP GINGER MUFFINS

2¹/₂ cups (375g) self-raising flour
¹/₂ teaspoon ground cloves
¹/₂ teaspoon mixed spice
¹/₄ cup (50g) brown sugar
1 tablespoon grated fresh ginger
1 cup (190g) Choc Bits
125g butter, melted
¹/₄ cup (60ml) golden syrup
2 eggs, lightly beaten
1 cup (250ml) milk

Grease 12 hole (¹/₃ cup/80ml capacity) muffin pan.

Sift dry ingredients into large bowl, stir in ginger and Choc Bits, then butter, golden syrup, eggs and milk. Spoon mixture into prepared pan. Bake muffins in moderately hot oven about 20 minutes.

Makes 12.

APRICOT BUTTERMILK MUFFINS

1½ cups (225g) roughly chopped dried apricots
¼ cup (60ml) brandy
3 cups (450g) self-raising flour
125g butter, chopped
½ cup (110g) caster sugar
2 eggs, lightly beaten
¾ cup (180ml) buttermilk

APRICOT BUTTER
60g butter
1 cup (160g) icing sugar mixture
1 tablespoon brandy

Grease 12 hole (⅓ cup/80ml capacity) muffin pan.

Combine apricots and brandy in bowl, stand 20 minutes. Process apricot mixture until finely chopped, reserve ¼ cup of apricot mixture. Sift flour into large bowl, rub in butter. Stir in sugar, apricot mixture, eggs and buttermilk. Spoon mixture into prepared pan. Bake in moderately hot oven about 20 minutes. Serve with apricot butter.

Apricot Butter: Beat butter in small bowl with electric mixer until as white as possible. Gradually beat in icing sugar, brandy and reserved apricot mixture.
Makes 12.

APPLE SPICE MUFFINS

2 cups (300g) self-raising flour
½ teaspoon bicarbonate of soda
½ teaspoon ground cinnamon
1 teaspoon ground ginger
¼ teaspoon ground nutmeg
pinch ground cloves
¼ cup (50g) brown sugar
½ x 410g can pie apples
1 egg, lightly beaten
¾ cup (180ml) milk
60g butter, melted
1 small (130g) apple
20g butter, melted, extra
2 tablespoons cinnamon sugar

Grease 6 hole (¾ cup/180ml capacity) muffin pan.

Sift flour, soda, spices and brown sugar into large bowl, stir in pie apples, then egg, milk and butter. Spoon mixture into prepared pan. Peel, core and halve apple, slice each half thinly. Place an apple slice on top of each muffin, brush with extra butter, sprinkle with cinnamon sugar. Bake in moderately hot oven about 25 minutes.
Makes 6.

BELOW: Apple Spice Muffins.
BELOW LEFT: Apricot Buttermilk Muffin.
LEFT: Choc Chip Ginger Muffins.

PROSCIUTTO, BASIL AND TOMATO MUFFINS

5 slices (75g) prosciutto
2½ cups (375g) self-raising flour
90g butter
1 egg, lightly beaten
1¼ cups (310ml) buttermilk
⅓ cup (80ml) milk
⅓ cup (50g) drained chopped
    sun-dried tomatoes
2 tablespoons chopped fresh basil
1 clove garlic, crushed
1 teaspoon cracked black pepper
1 tablespoon olive oil

Grease 6 hole (¾ cup/180ml capacity) muffin pan.

Cut prosciutto into strips. Sift flour into large bowl, rub in butter, stir in egg, buttermilk, milk, tomatoes, basil, garlic and pepper. Spoon mixture into pan, top with prosciutto, brush lightly with oil. Bake in moderately hot oven 20 minutes. Cover with foil, bake about a further 10 minutes.

Makes 6.

BUBBLE AND SQUEAK MUFFINS

We used leftover cauliflower, broccoli, zucchini and peppers in this recipe.

2½ cups (375g) self-raising flour
1 cup coarsely chopped
    cooked vegetables
1 medium (150g) carrot,
    coarsely grated
1 small (80g) onion, grated
2 tablespoons chopped fresh thyme
1 tablespoon chopped fresh
    flat leaf parsley
1½ cups (375ml) buttermilk
2 eggs, lightly beaten
90g butter, melted

MUSTARD BUTTER
¼ cup (55g) packaged soft
    cream cheese
90g butter, softened
2 teaspoons seeded mustard
1 teaspoon drained green
    peppercorns, crushed

Grease 6 hole (¾ cup/180ml capacity) muffin pan.

Sift flour into large bowl, add vegetables and herbs; stir in buttermilk, eggs and butter. Spoon mixture into prepared pan. Bake in moderately hot oven about 25 minutes.

Mustard Butter: Beat cream cheese and butter in small bowl until creamy, beat in mustard and peppercorns.

Makes 6.

ABOVE: Prosciutto, Basil and Tomato Muffins.
ABOVE RIGHT: Bubble and Squeak Muffins.
RIGHT: Pesto Salami Muffins.

PESTO SALAMI MUFFINS

2 cups (300g) self-raising flour
1½ cups (210g) chopped
    mild salami
⅓ cup (80ml) bottled pesto
3 eggs, lightly beaten
⅓ cup (80ml) vegetable oil
½ cup (125ml) buttermilk
⅔ cup (60g) grated gruyere cheese

PESTO CREAM
½ cup (125ml) sour cream
2 tablespoons bottled pesto

Grease 12 hole (⅓ cup/80ml capacity) muffin pan.

Sift flour into large bowl, stir in salami, pesto, eggs, oil and buttermilk. Spoon mixture into prepared pan, sprinkle with cheese. Bake in moderately hot oven about 20 minutes. Serve with pesto cream.

Pesto Cream: Combine ingredients in small bowl; mix well.

Makes 12.

PASSIONFRUIT, PINEAPPLE AND MINT MUFFINS

You will need about 4 passionfruit for this recipe.

2 cups (300g) self-raising flour
125g butter, chopped
2/3 cup (150g) caster sugar
2 tablespoons chopped fresh mint
1/2 cup (115g) chopped
    glace pineapple
1/4 cup (60ml) passionfruit pulp
1/2 cup (125ml) cream
2 eggs, lightly beaten

YOGURT CREAM
1/2 cup (125ml) cream
1/2 cup (125ml) plain yogurt
1 teaspoon grated orange rind
1 tablespoon passionfruit pulp

Grease 12 hole (1/3 cup/80ml capacity) muffin pan.

Sift flour into large bowl, rub in butter. Stir in sugar, mint, pineapple, passionfruit pulp, cream and eggs. Spoon mixture into prepared pan. Bake in moderately hot oven about 20 minutes. Serve muffins filled with yogurt cream.
Yogurt Cream: Combine cream and yogurt in small bowl, beat with electric mixer until soft peaks form. Fold in rind and passionfruit.

Makes 12.

HAZELNUT, FIG AND RICOTTA MUFFINS

2 1/2 cups (375g) self-raising flour
90g butter
3/4 cup (150g) firmly packed
    brown sugar
1 egg, lightly beaten
1 1/4 cups (310ml) buttermilk

FILLING
1/2 cup (95g) chopped dried figs
1/4 cup (60ml) water
1/2 cup (100g) ricotta cheese
1/4 cup (25g) packaged ground
    hazelnuts
1 tablespoon caster sugar
1/4 teaspoon ground cinnamon

Grease 6 hole (3/4 cup/180ml capacity) muffin pan.

Sift flour into large bowl, rub in butter. Stir in sugar, egg and buttermilk. Half-fill prepared pan with mixture, make a well in each muffin, drop rounded tablespoons of filling into wells, top with remaining muffin mixture. Bake in moderately hot oven about 30 minutes.
Filling: Combine figs and water in small pan, boil 2 minutes, drain; cool. Combine fig mixture with remaining ingredients in small bowl.

Makes 6.

CARAMEL NUT MUFFINS

2 cups (300g) self-raising flour
1/2 cup (110g) caster sugar
1 cup (170g) brazil nuts,
**   roughly chopped**
1 egg, lightly beaten
3/4 cup (180ml) milk, approximately
60g butter, melted
200g packet jersey caramels
12 brazil nuts, extra

Grease 12 hole (1/3 cup/80ml capacity) muffin pan.

Sift flour and sugar into large bowl, stir in nuts, egg, milk and butter. Spoon half the mixture into prepared pan. Place 2 caramels in centre of each muffin, top with remaining muffin mixture. Top each muffin with an extra nut. Bake in moderately hot oven about 20 minutes.

Makes 12.

ABOVE: Caramel Nut Muffins.
LEFT: Hazelnut, Fig and Ricotta Muffins.
ABOVE LEFT: Passionfruit, Pineapple and Mint Muffins.

HAM AND CHEESE MUFFINS

2 cups (300g) self-raising flour
1/2 teaspoon chicken stock powder
1/2 teaspoon ground hot paprika
80g butter
6 slices (130g) ham, chopped
1 1/2 cups (185g) coarsely grated
tasty cheddar cheese
1 egg, lightly beaten
1 cup (250ml) milk
ground hot paprika, extra

Grease 12 hole (1/3 cup/80ml capacity) muffin pan.

Sift dry ingredients into large bowl, rub in butter. Stir in ham and cheese, then egg and milk. Spoon mixture into prepared pan, sprinkle with a little extra paprika. Bake in moderately hot oven about 20 minutes.

Makes 12.

ASPARAGUS, SALMON AND MUSTARD MUFFINS

200g fresh asparagus
2 1/2 cups (375g) self-raising flour
2 eggs, lightly beaten
1 cup (250ml) buttermilk
2 tablespoons Dijon mustard
125g butter, melted
100g smoked salmon,
finely chopped

TOPPING
30g butter
1/4 cup (40g) chopped almonds
1 tablespoon finely grated
parmesan cheese
1 teaspoon drained green
peppercorns, crushed

Grease 12 hole (1/3 cup/80ml capacity) muffin pan.

Snap off and discard tough ends of asparagus. Boil, steam or microwave asparagus until just tender; drain, rinse under cold water, drain on absorbent paper; cool. Chop asparagus roughly.

Sift flour into large bowl, stir in eggs, buttermilk, mustard and butter, then asparagus and salmon. Spoon mixture into prepared pan, sprinkle with topping. Bake in moderately hot oven about 20 minutes.

Topping: Melt butter in small pan, add nuts, stir over heat until just beginning to brown. Stir in cheese and peppercorns.

Makes 12.

TANDOORI LAMB MUFFINS

250g lamb fillets, finely chopped
1/4 cup (60ml) plain yogurt
1 tablespoon tandoori paste
1/3 cup chopped fresh
coriander leaves
1 cup (150g) plain flour
1 1/2 cups (225g) self-raising flour
2 teaspoons ground coriander
1/4 cup (60ml) vegetable oil
2 eggs, lightly beaten
1 cup (250ml) milk

CUCUMBER YOGURT
3/4 cup (180ml) plain yogurt
2 medium (260g) Lebanese
cucumbers, seeded, chopped
1 tablespoon lime juice
2 teaspoons chopped fresh
coriander leaves

Grease 12 hole (1/3 cup/80ml capacity) muffin pan.

Combine lamb, yogurt, tandoori paste and 1 tablespoon of the fresh coriander in bowl, cover, refrigerate 2 hours.

Sift flours and ground coriander into large bowl, stir in lamb mixture, remaining fresh coriander, oil, eggs and milk. Spoon mixture into prepared pan. Bake in moderately hot oven about 20 minutes. Serve with cucumber yogurt.

Cucumber Yogurt: Combine all ingredients in small bowl; mix well.

Makes 12.

Setting from Accoutrement

Mugs from Opus Design

TOP: Tandoori Lamb Muffins.
ABOVE: Ham and Cheese Muffins.
LEFT: Asparagus, Salmon and Mustard Muffins.

MANGO STREUSEL MUFFINS

2¹/₃ cups (350g) self-raising flour
100g butter, chopped
1 cup (220g) caster sugar
1 cup (250ml) coconut milk
1 egg, lightly beaten
440g can mango slices in light
  syrup, drained, chopped

STREUSEL TOPPING
¹/₃ cup (50g) plain flour
50g butter
¹/₂ cup (80g) chopped almonds
¹/₄ cup (50g) brown sugar

Grease 12 hole (¹/₃ cup/80ml capacity) muffin pan.

Sift flour into large bowl, rub in butter. Stir in sugar, coconut milk and egg. Spoon mixture into prepared pan, top with mango, then streusel topping. Bake in moderately hot oven about 25 minutes.

Streusel Topping: Sift flour into small bowl, rub in butter, stir in nuts and sugar.

Makes 12.

MARMALADE ALMOND MUFFINS

2 cups (300g) self-raising flour
125g butter, chopped
1 cup (80g) flaked almonds
²/₃ cup (150g) caster sugar
1 tablespoon grated orange rind
¹/₂ cup (125ml) orange marmalade
2 eggs, lightly beaten
¹/₂ cup (125ml) milk
¹/₄ cup (20g) flaked almonds, extra

Grease 12 hole (¹/₃ cup/80ml capacity) muffin pan.

Sift flour into large bowl, rub in butter. Stir in nuts, sugar and rind, then marmalade, eggs and milk. Spoon mixture into prepared pan, sprinkle with extra nuts. Bake in moderately hot oven about 20 minutes.

Makes 12.

NUTTY CHOC CARAMEL MUFFINS

2¹/₂ cups (375g) self-raising flour
¹/₄ cup (25g) cocoa powder
³/₄ cup (150g) firmly packed
  brown sugar
2 x 60g Mars Bars, coarsely chopped
¹/₂ cup (85g) chopped brazil
  nuts, toasted
90g butter, melted
1 egg, lightly beaten
1¹/₄ cups (310ml) milk

Grease 12 hole (¹/₃ cup/80ml capacity) muffin pan.

Sift dry ingredients into large bowl, stir in remaining ingredients. Spoon mixture into prepared pan. Bake in moderately hot oven about 20 minutes.

Makes 12.

Cup from Home & Garden on the Mall

LEFT: Mango Streusel Muffins.
ABOVE: Marmalade Almond Muffins.
RIGHT: Nutty Choc Caramel Muffins.

CHERRY COCONUT MUFFINS

2 cups (300g) self-raising flour
125g butter, chopped
1 cup (70g) shredded coconut
1 cup (210g) red glace cherries,
    halved
2/3 cup (150g) caster sugar
270ml can coconut milk
1 egg, lightly beaten

Grease 12 hole (1/3 cup/80ml capacity) muffin pan.

Sift flour into large bowl, rub in butter. Stir in remaining ingredients. Spoon mixture into prepared pan. Bake in moderately hot oven about 20 minutes. Sprinkle with a little extra toasted shredded coconut and sifted icing sugar, if desired.

Makes 12.

CHOC BROWNIE MUFFINS

2 cups (300g) self-raising flour
1/3 cup (35g) cocoa powder
1/3 cup (75g) caster sugar
60g butter, melted
1/2 cup (95g) Choc Bits
1/2 cup (75g) chopped pistachios
1/2 cup (125ml) Nutella
1 egg, lightly beaten
3/4 cup (180ml) milk
1/2 cup (125ml) sour cream

Grease 12 hole (1/3 cup/80ml capacity) muffin pan.

Sift dry ingredients into large bowl, stir in remaining ingredients. Spoon mixture into prepared pan. Bake in moderately hot oven about 20 minutes.

Makes 12.

Tea setting from Mura Clay Gallery

PLUM AND PECAN WHOLEMEAL MUFFINS

1/2 x 825g can plums in natural juice
1 cup (150g) self-raising flour
2/3 cup (100g) wholemeal
    self-raising flour
1/2 teaspoon mixed spice
1/4 teaspoon ground cinnamon
90g butter
1/3 cup (75g) raw sugar
1/2 cup (60g) chopped pecans
1/2 cup (125ml) milk
1 egg, lightly beaten
1 tablespoon raw sugar, extra
1/4 teaspoon ground cinnamon,
    extra

Grease 6 hole (3/4 cup/180ml capacity) muffin pan.

Drain plums, stand on absorbent paper for 10 minutes; the juice is not needed for this recipe. Discard plum seeds, chop flesh roughly.

Sift flours and spices into large bowl, rub in butter. Stir in plums, sugar and nuts, then milk and egg. Spoon mixture into prepared pan, sprinkle with combined extra sugar and extra cinnamon. Bake in moderately hot oven about 25 minutes.

Makes 6.

Plate from The Bay Tree Kitchen Shop

LEFT: Choc Brownie Muffins.
FAR LEFT: Cherry Coconut Muffins.
ABOVE: Plum and Pecan
Wholemeal Muffin.

RHUBARB CRUMBLE MUFFINS

2½ cups (375g) self-raising flour
⅔ cup (130g) firmly packed
   brown sugar
100g butter, melted
1 cup (250ml) milk
1 egg, lightly beaten

FILLING
1½ cups (190g) chopped
   fresh rhubarb
¼ cup (55g) caster sugar
2 tablespoons water
¼ teaspoon grated lemon rind

CRUMBLE TOPPING
¼ cup (35g) plain flour
⅓ cup (65g) firmly packed
   brown sugar
2 tablespoons toasted muesli
1 teaspoon grated lemon rind
30g butter, melted

Grease 12 hole (⅓ cup/80ml capacity) muffin pan.

Sift dry ingredients into large bowl, stir in remaining ingredients. Half-fill prepared pan with muffin mixture, make a well in each muffin, spoon filling into wells, top with remaining muffin mixture, spread carefully to cover filling. Sprinkle with crumble topping, press gently onto muffin mixture. Bake in moderately hot oven about 20 minutes.
Filling: Combine all ingredients in small pan, bring to boil, simmer, uncovered, about 5 minutes or until mixture is thick and rhubarb soft; cool.
Crumble Topping: Combine all ingredients in small bowl; mix well.

Makes 12.

CHOCOLATE, RUM AND RAISIN MUFFINS

1 cup (170g) raisins, chopped
¼ cup (60ml) dark rum
1⅔ cups (250g) self-raising flour
⅓ cup (35g) cocoa powder
½ cup (110g) caster sugar
1 cup (190g) Choc Bits
60g butter, melted
¾ cup (180ml) milk
1 egg, lightly beaten

Combine raisins and rum in small bowl, cover, stand 1 hour. Grease 12 hole (⅓ cup/80ml) capacity muffin pan.

Sift dry ingredients into large bowl, stir in raisin mixture and remaining ingredients. Spoon mixture into prepared pan. Bake in moderately hot oven about 20 minutes.

Makes 12.

CARROT WALNUT MUFFINS

You need about 2 medium (240g) carrots for this recipe.

2½ cups (375g) self-raising flour
1½ teaspoons ground cinnamon
¼ teaspoon ground nutmeg
½ cup (110g) caster sugar
2 teaspoons grated orange rind
½ cup (60g) chopped walnuts
1 cup coarsely grated carrots
1 tablespoon orange marmalade
½ cup (125ml) vegetable oil
2 eggs, lightly beaten
¾ cup (180ml) orange juice
¼ cup (60ml) milk
12 walnut halves

CREAM CHEESE TOPPING
125g packet cream cheese
¼ cup (40g) icing sugar mixture
1 teaspoon vanilla essence

Grease 12 hole (⅓ cup/80ml capacity) muffin pan.

Sift dry ingredients into large bowl. Stir in rind, chopped nuts and carrots, then marmalade, oil, eggs, juice and milk. Spoon mixture into prepared pan. Bake in moderately hot oven about 15 minutes. Serve muffins topped with cream cheese topping and halved nuts.
Cream Cheese Topping: Beat all ingredients in small bowl with electric mixer until light and fluffy.

Makes 12.

ABOVE: Rhubarb Crumble Muffins.
TOP: Chocolate, Rum and Raisin Muffins.
RIGHT: Carrot Walnut Muffins.

Footed bowl from Home & Garden on the Mall

PINEAPPLE GINGER MUFFINS

2 cups (300g) self-raising flour
1 teaspoon ground ginger
125g butter, chopped
2/3 cup (150g) caster sugar
1 cup (90g) coconut
1/2 cup (115g) chopped glace ginger
**1/2 cup (115g) chopped glace
   pineapple**
2/3 cup (160ml) milk
2 eggs, lightly beaten
. 1/4 cup (60ml) golden syrup

GINGER CREAM
300ml thickened cream
3 teaspoons caster sugar
**1 tablespoon finely chopped
   glace ginger**

Grease 12 hole (1/3 cup/80ml capacity)
muffin pan.

Sift flour and ground ginger into
large bowl, rub in butter. Stir in sugar,
coconut, glace ginger and pineapple,
then milk, eggs and golden syrup.
Spoon mixture into prepared pan.
Bake in moderately hot oven about
20 minutes. Serve with ginger cream.
Ginger Cream: Beat cream and sugar
together in small bowl until thick, stir
in ginger.

Makes 12.

JAM AND CREAM MUFFINS

*Use the nuts and jam of your choice
in this recipe; we used brazil nuts
and blackberry jam. Be careful of the
hot jam when turning muffins onto
a wire rack to cool.*

2½ cups (375g) self-raising flour
½ cup (110g) caster sugar
90g butter, melted
½ cup (85g) chopped nuts
1 egg, lightly beaten
1 cup (250ml) cream
¼ cup (60ml) milk
½ cup (125ml) jam

Grease 12 hole (⅓ cup/80ml capacity)
muffin pan.

Sift dry ingredients into large bowl,
stir in butter, nuts, egg, cream and milk.
Half-fill prepared pan with mixture,
make a well in each muffin, drop
rounded teaspoons of jam into wells,
top with remaining muffin mixture. Bake
in moderately hot oven about 20 minutes.

Makes 12.

COFFEE HAZELNUT MUFFINS

2 cups (300g) self-raising flour
¾ cup (105g) plain flour
⅓ cup (35g) packaged ground
     hazelnuts
1 cup (200g) firmly packed
     brown sugar
1½ tablespoons coffee powder
1 tablespoon boiling water
2 tablespoons Nutella
2 eggs, lightly beaten
1½ cups (375ml) buttermilk
¾ cup (180ml) vegetable oil

HAZELNUT FROSTING
1 cup (160g) icing sugar mixture
1 tablespoon cocoa powder
2 tablespoons Nutella
40g butter, softened
1 tablespoon milk

Grease 12 hole (⅓ cup/80ml capacity)
muffin pan.

Sift flours into large bowl, stir in
ground nuts and sugar, combined
coffee and water, Nutella, eggs, buttermilk and oil. Spoon mixture into prepared pan. Bake in moderately hot
oven about 20 minutes. Spread cold
muffins with hazelnut frosting.
Hazelnut Frosting: Sift icing sugar
and cocoa into small bowl, stir in
remaining ingredients.

Makes 12.

Plates from Mura Clay Gallery

ABOVE: Pineapple Ginger Muffins.
LEFT: Jam and Cream Muffins.
TOP LEFT: Coffee Hazelnut Muffins.

Breads

All of our delicious breads are made with step-by-step recipes. Some of these recipes use yeast, but even novice cooks shouldn't be deterred from using yeast. It is simply a raising or leavening agent. Baking powder is also used for leavening. Bread with no raising is known as "unleavened".

■ You can use dry (dried) yeast or fresh compressed yeast. We use dry yeast packaged in 5 x 7g sachets (2 teaspoons per sachet). Bulk dry yeast is available in 500g or 1kg vacuum-sealed packs; it will keep in a cool, dry place for up to 1 year, if unopened. Store in the refrigerator in an airtight container after opening.

■ Generally, 2 teaspoons (7g) of dry yeast is equivalent to 15g of compressed yeast, but it is a good idea to read and follow the instructions on the packet.

■ Fresh compressed yeast has a limited shelf life and must be stored in the refrigerator in an airtight container.

■ Liquid added to yeast should be warm, about 26°C. An easy "rule of thumb" method for those without a thermometer is to add 1/3 boiling liquid to 2/3 cold. If liquid is too cold, it will retard the yeast growth; if too hot, it will kill the action of the yeast.

■ Gluten is important in bread-making as it is the protein in flour which gives elasticity to the dough. However, if you are allergic to gluten, try our gluten-free bread.

KNEADING

■ Kneading makes the dough smooth, pliable and elastic. Start by scraping the dough from the bowl onto a lightly floured surface in front of you.

■ Now press the heel of 1 hand gently but firmly into the lump of dough and p-u-u-sh it away from you. Lift the furthest edge of the dough a little, give the dough a quarter turn, fold the dough in half towards you, and repeat the press-and-push motion. Keep going for the time specified. When kneaded sufficiently, dough will spring back if pressed with a finger.

PROVING

■ An important step is proving the dough, or giving it time to rise after kneading. Place the dough in an oiled bowl, turn dough lightly to grease top and prevent a skin forming. Cover bowl with a clean cloth or plastic wrap and stand it in a warm place away from draughts until risen as specified.

■ Refrigerating retards proving. Place the kneaded dough, covered, in the refrigerator for up to 12 hours or until risen as specified.

Breadboards and wire basket from The Bay Tree Kitchen shop; tiles from Country Floors

FREEZING

■ Large unbaked loaves are not satisfactory to freeze at home.

■ Small breads such as dinner rolls, pizza bases and unglazed sweet buns are suitable to freeze if partly baked. Follow the recipe, but bake for only half the time, cool on the oven tray, then freeze, uncovered, on the tray until firm. Transfer to freezer wrap or freezer bags before storing in the freezer; press bag gently or use a freezer pump to expel all the air. Such products can be frozen for up to 3 months.

■ To complete baking, thaw completely at room temperature and continue baking as specified in the recipe.

■ To freeze baked loaves, cool bread as quickly as possible, pack in good-quality freezer bags, expel all air, and freeze as quickly as possible. It can be a good idea to slice the bread first so you can take out just the amount you want. Correctly wrapped baked bread can be frozen for up to 2 months.

OVEN HINTS

■ Always check the manufacturer's instructions for your particular oven. As a guide, the top of the baked product should be in the centre of the oven; 220°C is the perfect temperature for baking bread.

■ Sweet breads are baked at slightly lower temperatures. Cover bread loosely with foil if overbrowning.

■ To test if bread is cooked, tap bread firmly on the bottom crust with fingers; if it sounds hollow it is cooked. You will need to turn the bread out of the pan onto a tea-towel, tap quickly, and return to pan for further baking, if necessary. Work with caution, as bread will be very hot.

■ Recipes are unsuitable to microwave.

Clockwise from top left: Brown Bread; French Sticks; Cottage Loaf; White Bread; Dinner Rolls (recipes over page).

2. Sift flour and salt into large bowl, stir in butter, milk and yeast mixture. Turn dough onto floured surface, knead about 10 minutes or until dough is smooth and elastic.

3. Place dough into greased bowl, cover, stand in warm place about 1 hour or until mixture has doubled in size.

WHITE BREAD

3 teaspoons (10g) dry yeast
1/2 cup (125ml) warm water
2 teaspoons sugar
2 1/2 cups (375g) plain flour
1 teaspoon salt
30g butter, melted
1/2 cup (125ml) warm milk

1. Combine yeast, water and sugar in small bowl, whisk until yeast is dissolved. Cover, stand in warm place about 10 minutes or until mixture is frothy.

4. Turn dough onto floured surface, knead until smooth, roll dough to 18cm x 35cm rectangle, roll up from short side like a Swiss roll, place into greased 14cm x 21cm loaf pan. Cover, stand in warm place about 20 minutes or until risen. Bake in moderately hot oven about 45 minutes. Turn bread onto wire rack to cool.

VARIATIONS

BROWN BREAD: Substitute half the plain flour with wholemeal plain flour. You may need to mix in a little more warm milk to make a firm dough.

FRENCH STICKS: Starting at Step 4: Divide dough in half, shape each half into 40cm sausage, place onto 2 greased oven trays, cover, stand in warm place about 15 minutes or until dough has almost doubled in size. Using a sharp knife, make 5 long slashes on bread sticks. Sprinkle each stick with about a tablespoon of plain flour. Bake in moderately hot oven about 20 minutes.

COTTAGE LOAF: Starting at Step 4: Shape dough into 20cm round, place onto greased oven tray, cover, stand in warm place about 15 minutes or until almost doubled in size. Using a sharp knife, make slashes in criss-cross pattern on top of bread, sprinkle with about a tablespoon of plain flour. Bake in moderately hot oven about 30 minutes.

DINNER ROLLS: Starting at Step 4: Divide dough into 12 portions, shape into 8cm rolls. Place rolls onto greased oven trays, cover, stand in warm place about 15 minutes or until almost doubled in size. Using a sharp knife, make slashes on rolls. Brush rolls with milk, sprinkle with seeds, if desired. Bake in moderately hot oven about 20 minutes.

Chapati bowl and rolling pins from Accoutrement

CHAPATIS

Be aware that chapatis need to be cooked over a flame to achieve the blistered appearance.

1 cup (150g) white plain flour
1 cup (160g) wholemeal plain flour
1 teaspoon salt
20g ghee
3/4 cup (180ml) warm water,
approximately

2. Divide dough into 14 portions. Roll portions on floured surface into 20cm rounds, cover with a cloth, stand 10 minutes before cooking.

4. Place uncooked side of chapati directly over medium flame, checking frequently until chapati begins to blister. Repeat with remaining rounds. Wrap cooked chapatis in a cloth to keep warm or serve while warm.

Makes 14.

1. Sift flours and salt into large bowl, rub in ghee. Add enough water to mix to a firm dough. Turn dough onto floured surface, knead about 10 minutes, working in about an extra 1/4 cup (35g) plain white flour. Cover dough with cloth, stand 1 hour.

3. Heat griddle or heavy-based frying pan until very hot, cook 1 round at a time, for about 30 seconds on first side or until round just begins to colour; remove from pan.

OLIVE BREAD WITH SAGE AND OREGANO

4 teaspoons (14g) dry yeast
1 teaspoon sugar
1¼ cups (310ml) warm milk
1 cup (250ml) warm water
2 cups (300g) plain flour
⅓ cup (80ml) olive oil
3½ cups (525g) plain flour, extra
1 teaspoon salt
1¼ cups (150g) seeded black olives, halved
2 tablespoons shredded fresh sage
2 tablespoons chopped fresh oregano

1. Combine yeast, sugar, milk and water in large bowl, whisk until yeast is dissolved.

2. Whisk in sifted flour, cover, stand in warm place about 30 minutes or until mixture is doubled in size.

3. Stir in oil, then sifted extra flour and salt. Turn dough onto floured surface, knead about 10 minutes or until dough is smooth and elastic. Place dough in large greased bowl, cover, stand in warm place about 1 hour or until dough has doubled in size.

4. Turn dough onto floured surface, knead in remaining ingredients.

5. Roll dough to 30cm x 35cm oval. Fold dough almost in half, transfer to large greased oven tray, shape dough into an oval. Cover dough, stand in warm place about 45 minutes or until dough has increased in size by half. Sift about another 2 tablespoons of flour over bread, bake in moderately hot oven about 45 minutes.

Basket from House

CRUSTY GARLIC LOAF

2 teaspoons (7g) dry yeast
1 teaspoon sugar
1 cup (250ml) warm milk
4½ cups (675g) plain flour
1 teaspoon salt
¼ cup (40g) cornmeal
4 cloves garlic, crushed
40g butter, softened
1 tablespoon olive oil
1 cup (250ml) warm milk,
    extra, approximately

1. Combine yeast, sugar and milk in small bowl, whisk until yeast is dissolved. Cover, stand in warm place about 10 minutes or until mixture is frothy.

2. Sift flour and salt into large bowl, add yeast mixture, cornmeal, garlic, butter, oil and enough extra milk to mix to a soft dough.

3. Turn dough onto floured surface, knead about 10 minutes or until dough is smooth and elastic.

4. Place dough into greased bowl, cover, stand in warm place about 1¼ hours or until dough has doubled in size.

5. Knead dough on floured surface until smooth, place on greased oven tray, shape into 35cm loaf; sprinkle with a little extra cornmeal. Cut slashes on top of loaf, cover with tea-towel; stand in warm place about 20 minutes or until slightly risen. Bake in hot oven 10 minutes, reduce heat to moderate, bake about a further 30 minutes. Lift onto wire rack to cool.

Wire basket from The Bay Tree Kitchen Shop

JAM DOUGHNUTS

4 teaspoons (14g) dry yeast
1¼ cups (310ml) warm milk
¼ cup (55g) caster sugar
60g butter, melted
2 eggs, lightly beaten
3¾ cups (560g) plain flour
⅓ cup (80ml) strawberry jam
vegetable oil for deep-frying
½ cup (110g) caster sugar, extra

1. Combine yeast, milk and sugar in bowl, whisk until yeast is dissolved. Cover, stand in warm place about 10 minutes or until mixture is frothy.

2. Whisk butter and eggs into yeast mixture. Sift flour into large bowl, stir in yeast mixture, mix to a soft dough. Cover, stand in warm place about 45 minutes or until dough has doubled in size.

3. Turn dough onto floured surface, knead dough about 10 minutes or until smooth and elastic, but still slightly sticky. Roll dough out to 1cm thickness, cut into 5.5cm rounds. Place a teaspoon of jam on half the rounds, top with remaining rounds, press edges together with fingers.

4. Place rounds on greased oven trays, cover, stand in warm place about 10 minutes or until rounds have almost doubled in size, press edges together again, if necessary.

5. Deep-fry doughnuts in batches in hot oil until golden brown and cooked through. Drain on absorbent paper, toss in extra sugar.
Makes about 20.

China from Accoutrement; tiles from Country Floors

KUGELHUPF

2 teaspoons (7g) dry yeast
1 teaspoon caster sugar
½ cup (125ml) warm milk
½ cup (75g) plain flour
150g butter
1 teaspoon vanilla essence
½ cup (110g) caster sugar, extra
½ teaspoon salt
3 eggs
3 cups (450g) plain flour, extra

WALNUT FILLING
30g butter, melted
1½ tablespoons warm milk
1 teaspoon coffee powder
¾ cup (75g) walnuts, toasted,
finely chopped
¼ cup (50g) brown sugar
2 teaspoons grated lemon rind
2 tablespoons stale breadcrumbs
1 teaspoon mixed spice
½ teaspoon ground ginger

1. Combine yeast, sugar and milk in large bowl, whisk until yeast is dissolved. Stir in flour, cover, stand in a warm place about 40 minutes or until mixture has doubled in size.

2. Beat butter, essence, extra sugar and salt in small bowl with electric mixer until light and creamy, beat in eggs 1 at a time.

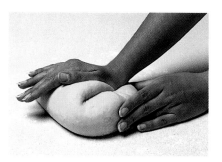

3. Stir butter mixture and sifted extra flour into yeast mixture in 2 batches. Turn dough onto floured surface, knead about 10 minutes or until smooth and elastic. Place dough in large greased bowl, cover, stand in warm place about 1½ hours or until doubled in size.

4. Turn dough onto floured surface, knead until smooth. Roll dough to 20cm x 40cm rectangle. Spread walnut filling over dough, roll up from long side as for Swiss roll. Brush 1 end of roll with water.

5. Grease and flour 21cm baba pan. Place roll in pan, seam towards centre of pan. Gently press dough into pan; press ends together to join. Cover pan, stand in warm place until dough is risen to within 1cm from rim of pan. Bake in moderately hot oven 10 minutes, reduce heat to moderate, bake about 40 minutes. Serve dusted with icing sugar, if desired.

6. Walnut Filling: Combine butter, milk and coffee in small bowl; mix well. Stir in remaining ingredients.

BRIOCHE

4 teaspoons (14g) dry yeast
1/3 cup (80ml) warm water
1/4 cup (55g) caster sugar
4 cups (600g) plain flour
1 teaspoon salt
5 eggs, lightly beaten
250g butter
1 egg, lightly beaten, extra
1 tablespoon sugar

1. Combine yeast, water and 1 tablespoon of the caster sugar in small bowl, whisk until yeast is dissolved. Cover, stand in warm place about 10 minutes or until mixture is frothy.

2. Sift flour, remaining caster sugar and salt into large bowl, add yeast mixture and eggs, stir until just combined. Turn dough onto floured surface, knead about 10 minutes or until dough is smooth and elastic.

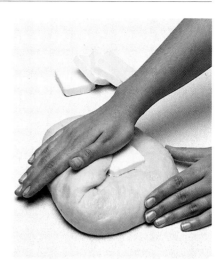

3. Divide butter into 10 portions, knead each portion into dough, kneading well after each addition until all the butter is incorporated and dough is smooth and glossy. Place dough in large bowl, cover, refrigerate overnight.

4. Divide dough into 3 equal portions, shape into 45cm sausages. Place sausages on large greased oven tray, plait sausages, cover, stand in cool place about 1 hour or until dough has nearly doubled in size. Brush plait with extra egg, sprinkle with sugar. Bake in moderately hot oven 10 minutes, reduce heat to moderate, bake about a further 15 minutes.

Setting from Accoutrement

2. Sift flour and salt into large bowl. Stir in milk, butter and yeast mixture, mix to a soft dough.

3. Turn dough onto floured surface, knead about 5 minutes or until smooth and elastic. Place dough in oiled bowl, cover; stand in warm place about 1 hour or until dough has almost doubled in size.

4. Turn dough onto floured surface, knead until smooth. Shape dough into 20cm x 26cm rectangle. Brush with extra butter, spread evenly with Nutella, leaving a 1cm border; sprinkle with combined extra sugar and cinnamon. Roll up from short side, like a Swiss roll. Place into greased 14cm x 21cm loaf pan, cover with plastic wrap, stand in warm place about 40 minutes or until dough has doubled in size. Remove plastic. Bake in moderately hot oven 10 minutes, reduce heat to moderate, bake about 25 minutes.

CINNAMON SPIRAL LOAF

2 teaspoons (7g) dry yeast
¼ teaspoon sugar
½ cup (125ml) warm water
3 cups (450g) plain flour
1 teaspoon salt
⅔ cup (160ml) warm milk
40g butter, melted
2 teaspoons butter, melted, extra
⅓ cup (80ml) Nutella
2 teaspoons sugar, extra
1 teaspoon ground cinnamon

1. Combine yeast, sugar and water in small bowl, whisk until yeast is dissolved, cover, stand in warm place about 10 minutes or until mixture is frothy.

Bread knife from The Bay Tree Kitchen Shop

CHILLI CORN BREAD

1 cup (150g) self-raising flour
1 teaspoon salt
1 cup (170g) cornmeal
1/2 cup (100g) kibbled rye
1 tablespoon brown sugar
1 teaspoon ground cumin
2 tablespoons chopped
    fresh parsley
1 teaspoon chopped fresh thyme
1/2 cup (60g) grated tasty
    cheddar cheese
310g can creamed corn
2/3 cup (90g) frozen corn
    kernels, thawed
2/3 cup (160ml) buttermilk
1/3 cup (80ml) milk
2 teaspoons sambal oelek
2 eggs, lightly beaten
50g butter, melted

1. Grease deep 19cm square cake pan, line base with baking paper. Sift flour and salt into large bowl, stir in cornmeal, rye, sugar, cumin, herbs and cheese.

2. Combine remaining ingredients in medium bowl; mix well, stir into dry ingredients.

3. Spread mixture into prepared pan, bake in moderately hot oven about 1 hour. Stand, covered, 10 minutes before turning onto wire rack to cool.

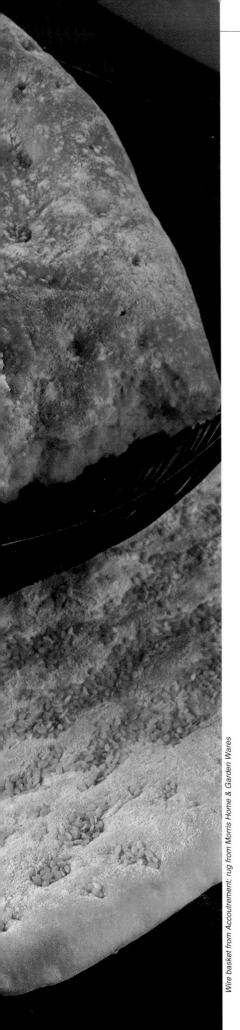

TURKISH BREAD

STARTER
½ teaspoon dry yeast
¼ cup (60ml) warm water
2 tablespoons warm milk
1 cup (150g) plain flour

DOUGH
1 teaspoon dry yeast
1½ cups (375ml) warm water
1 teaspoon sugar
3 cups (450g) plain flour
1½ teaspoons salt
2 tablespoons olive oil
2 teaspoons sesame seeds

1. Starter: Combine yeast, water and milk in small bowl, whisk until yeast is dissolved; stir in flour. Cover, stand in warm place 6 hours or overnight.

2. Dough: Combine yeast, water and sugar in small bowl, whisk until yeast is dissolved. Cover, stand in warm place about 10 minutes or until mixture is slightly foamy.

3. Turn starter onto floured surface, knead 2 minutes or until smooth. Cut starter into 2cm pieces. Sift flour and salt into large bowl, add yeast mixture, starter pieces and oil, mix to a soft dough. Turn dough onto floured surface, knead about 2 minutes or until almost smooth. Place dough into greased bowl, cover, stand in warm place about 40 minutes or until doubled in size.

4. Turn dough onto floured surface, knead until smooth. Halve dough, knead each half for about 5 minutes or until smooth and elastic. Place each half of dough into greased bowl, cover, stand in warm place about 40 minutes or until almost doubled in size.

5. Roll each half of dough into an oval about 35cm long. Make indents evenly over dough with your finger; dust with a little flour, sprinkle with seeds. Cover bread with greased plastic wrap to prevent drying out while oven trays are being heated.

Now place lightly greased oven trays in a very hot oven 3 minutes. Quickly remove plastic from bread, quickly place bread onto hot trays. Bake in very hot oven about 12 minutes.

Makes 2.

Wire basket from Accoutrement; rug from Morris Home & Garden Wares

SPINACH AND FETA PIZZA

2 teaspoons (7g) dry yeast
1 teaspoon sugar
2½ cups (375g) plain flour
1 cup (250ml) warm water
½ teaspoon salt
2 tablespoons olive oil
¼ cup (40g) semolina
1 bunch (500g) English spinach
1 cup (200g) feta cheese, crumbled
10 (100g) cherry tomatoes, halved
⅓ cup (25g) grated parmesan cheese

TOMATO SAUCE
1 tablespoon olive oil
1 medium (150g) onion, chopped
2 cloves garlic, crushed
425g can tomatoes
½ cup (125ml) tomato paste
¼ cup chopped fresh basil
1 teaspoon sugar

1. Combine yeast, sugar, 1 tablespoon of the flour and water in small bowl, whisk until yeast is dissolved. Cover, stand in warm place about 10 minutes or until mixture is frothy. Combine remaining sifted flour and salt in processor, pour in combined yeast mixture and oil while motor is operating. Process until dough forms a ball.

2. Turn dough onto floured surface, knead about 5 minutes or until dough is smooth and elastic. Place dough in large greased bowl, cover, stand in warm place about 1 hour or until dough has doubled in size.

3. Turn dough onto surface sprinkled with half the semolina, knead 1 minute. Place dough on large oven tray sprinkled with remaining semolina; press dough into a 32cm square.

4. Boil, steam or microwave spinach until wilted. Drain spinach; chop finely. Spread pizza base with tomato sauce, leaving a 3cm border. Top with spinach and remaining ingredients. Bake in very hot oven about 20 minutes.

5. Tomato Sauce: Heat oil in pan, add onion and garlic, cook, stirring, until onion is soft. Stir in undrained crushed tomatoes, paste, basil and sugar, simmer, uncovered, about 5 minutes or until thickened.

Glassware and pizza cutter from House

MIXED GRAIN LOAF

1/4 cup (50g) cracked buckwheat
1/2 cup (80g) burghul
1/4 cup (50g) kibbled rye
3 teaspoons (10g) dry yeast
1 teaspoon sugar
3/4 cup (180ml) warm milk
1/4 cup (60ml) warm water
2 1/4 cups (335g) white plain flour
1/2 cup (80g) wholemeal plain flour
1 teaspoon salt
1 tablespoon linseeds
2 teaspoons olive oil
1 egg yolk
1 teaspoon milk, extra
2 teaspoons sesame seeds
2 teaspoons cracked
    buckwheat, extra

1. Place buckwheat, burghul and kibbled rye in small heatproof bowl, cover with boiling water, cover, stand 30 minutes. Rinse well, drain well.

2. Combine yeast, sugar, milk and water in small bowl, whisk until yeast is dissolved. Cover, stand in warm place about 10 minutes or until mixture is frothy.

3. Sift flours and salt into large bowl, add grain mixture and linseeds. Stir in oil and yeast mixture; mix to a soft dough. Turn dough onto floured surface, knead about 10 minutes or until dough is smooth and elastic. Place dough in large greased bowl, cover, stand in warm place about 1 hour or until dough has doubled in size.

4. Turn dough onto floured surface, knead until smooth. Divide dough into 3 pieces. Shape each piece into a 30cm sausage. Plait sausages, place into greased 14cm x 21cm loaf pan. Cover, stand in warm place about 30 minutes or until risen.

5. Brush dough with combined egg yolk and extra milk, sprinkle evenly with combined sesame seeds and extra buckwheat. Bake in moderately hot oven about 45 minutes.

Setting from The Bay Tree Kitchen Shop

GLUTEN-FREE BREAD

3 cups (450g) gluten-free plain flour
2 teaspoons gluten-free
 baking powder
1½ teaspoons salt
1½ cups (180g) oat bran
1 cup (160g) sunflower seed kernels
70g butter, chopped
1½ cups (375ml) milk
2 eggs, lightly beaten
2 teaspoons poppy seeds

1. Sift flour, baking powder and salt into large bowl; stir in oat bran and kernels.

2. Rub in butter; stir in combined milk and eggs; do not overmix.

3. Press mixture into greased 14cm x 21cm loaf pan; do not smooth top. Brush with a little extra milk, sprinkle with seeds. Bake in moderate oven about 1 hour. Stand bread 10 minutes before turning onto wire rack to cool.

Setting from The Bay Tree Kitchen Shop

PAGNOTTA

2 teaspoons (7g) dry yeast
1/2 teaspoon sugar
1/2 cup (125ml) warm water
3 1/2 cups (525g) plain flour
1 teaspoon salt
1 tablespoon olive oil
3/4 cup (180ml) warm water, extra
1/4 cup (60ml) warm milk,
    approximately
1 teaspoon salt, extra

1. Combine yeast, sugar and water in small bowl, whisk until yeast is dissolved. Cover bowl, stand in warm place about 20 minutes or until mixture is frothy.

2. Sift flour and salt into large bowl, add yeast mixture, oil, extra water and enough milk to mix to a soft dough. Turn dough onto floured surface, knead about 2 minutes or until smooth. Place dough in oiled bowl, turn dough to coat all over with oil. Cover, stand in warm place about 30 minutes or until dough has doubled in size.

3. Turn dough onto floured surface, knead about 5 minutes or until smooth and elastic. Shape dough into a 58cm sausage, shape sausage into a ring on greased and floured oven tray, brush ends with water; press together gently. Place extra salt in small bowl, stir in 2 teaspoons of hot water. Brush pagnotta with salt mixture, sprinkle with a little extra flour. Place pagnotta in cold oven, turn temperature to moderately hot, bake about 40 minutes. Lift onto wire rack to cool.

FRUIT AND NUT LOAF

2 teaspoons (7g) dry yeast
1/4 cup (55g) caster sugar
2 tablespoons warm water
2/3 cup (160ml) warm milk
1 cup (150g) plain flour
1 egg, lightly beaten
2 teaspoons grated orange rind
2 cups (300g) plain flour, extra
1 teaspoon salt
1/2 teaspoon ground cinnamon
100g butter, softened
1/4 cup (40g) sultanas
1/4 cup (40g) raisins
1/4 cup (35g) dried currants
1/4 cup (30g) chopped
** walnuts, toasted**
1 egg yolk
1 tablespoon caster sugar, extra
1/2 teaspoon ground
** cinnamon, extra**

1. Grease 14cm x 21cm loaf pan, line base with baking paper. Combine yeast, 2 teaspoons of the sugar and water in large bowl, whisk until yeast is dissolved. Whisk in milk and sifted flour. Cover, stand in warm place about 30 minutes or until mixture is frothy.

2. Stir in egg and rind, then sifted extra flour, salt, cinnamon and remaining sugar. Stir in butter, fruit and nuts.

3. Turn dough onto floured surface, knead until smooth. Place dough into greased bowl, cover, stand in warm place about 1 1/2 hours or until dough has doubled in size.

4. Turn dough onto floured surface, knead until smooth, place into prepared pan. Cover loosely with greased plastic wrap, stand in warm place about 30 minutes or until risen slightly. Remove plastic wrap. Brush loaf with egg yolk, sprinkle with combined extra sugar and extra cinnamon. Bake in moderately hot oven 10 minutes, reduce heat to moderate, bake about a further 30 minutes. Turn onto wire rack to cool.

China from Accoutrement; butter pats from The Bay Tree Kitchen Shop

E AND BACON ROLLS

oons (14g) dry yeast
poon sugar
ups (375ml) warm water
5 cups (750g) plain flour
2 teaspoons salt
1/2 cup (125ml) milk
2 tablespoons sugar, extra
60g butter, melted
1 egg, lightly beaten
1 tablespoon milk, extra
1 1/4 cups (155g) grated tasty
   cheddar cheese
4 bacon rashers, finely chopped

1. Combine yeast, sugar and water in small bowl, whisk until yeast is dissolved. Cover bowl, stand in warm place about 10 minutes or until mixture is frothy.

2. Sift flour and salt into large bowl. Stir in yeast mixture, milk, extra sugar and butter, mix to a soft dough. Knead on floured surface about 5 minutes or until smooth and elastic. Place dough into greased bowl, cover; stand in warm place about 30 minutes or until dough has doubled in size.

3. Turn dough onto floured surface, knead until smooth. Divide dough into 16 portions, roll each portion into a 10cm x 12cm oval. Place onto lightly greased oven trays, cover with greased plastic wrap, stand in warm place about 15 minutes or until rolls are well risen.

4. Remove plastic wrap. Brush rolls with combined egg and extra milk, sprinkle evenly with cheese and bacon. Bake in moderately hot oven about 20 minutes.

Makes 16.

...OSS BUNS

...oons (14g) dry yeast
... (55g) caster sugar
1 cup (250ml) warm milk
4 cups (600g) plain flour
1 teaspoon ground cinnamon
60g butter
1 egg, lightly beaten
1/2 cup (125ml) warm water
3/4 cup (110g) dried currants
1/4 cup (40g) mixed peel
1 tablespoon apricot jam

FLOUR PASTE
1/2 cup (75g) plain flour
1 tablespoon caster sugar
1/3 cup (80ml) water

1. Combine yeast, sugar and milk in small bowl, whisk until yeast is dissolved. Cover bowl, stand in warm place about 10 minutes or until mixture is frothy.

2. Sift flour and cinnamon into large bowl, rub in butter. Stir in yeast mixture, egg, water and fruit, cover, stand in warm place about 1 hour or until mixture has doubled in size.

3. Turn dough onto floured surface, knead about 5 minutes or until smooth and elastic. Divide dough into 16 portions, knead into balls. Place buns in greased 23cm square slab cake pan, stand in warm place about 20 minutes or until dough has risen to top of pan.

4. Place flour paste into piping bag fitted with small plain tube, pipe crosses onto buns. Bake in moderately hot oven 10 minutes, reduce heat to moderate, bake about a further 15 minutes. Turn buns onto wire rack, brush with warmed sieved jam.

5. Flour Paste: Combine flour and sugar in small bowl, gradually blend in water; stir until smooth.
Makes 16.

ICED FINGER BUNS

4 teaspoons (14g) dry yeast
2 tablespoons caster sugar
2 tablespoons honey
1 cup (250ml) warm milk
4 cups (600g) plain flour
80g butter
½ cup (125ml) warm water
1 teaspoon vanilla essence
1 egg, lightly beaten
¾ cup (120g) sultanas
¼ cup (40g) mixed peel
½ cup (35g) shredded coconut

GLAZE
¼ cup (60ml) apricot jam
1 teaspoon gelatine
2 teaspoons water

ICING
1 cup (160g) icing sugar mixture
20g butter
2 teaspoons water, approximately

ICED TEACAKES

To make 2 delicious teacakes, you will need 1 quantity of ingredients for the basic mixture, as above. Prepare dough up to Step 2. Turn dough onto floured surface, knead about 5 minutes or until smooth. Halve dough and shape into 2 x 20cm round teacakes. Bake teacakes in hot oven about 15 minutes. You will need 2 quantities of icing and glaze for them.

1. Combine yeast, sugar, honey and milk in small bowl; whisk until yeast is dissolved. Cover bowl, stand in warm place about 10 minutes or until mixture is frothy.

2. Sift flour into large bowl, rub in butter. Stir in yeast mixture, water, essence, egg and fruit, mix to a soft dough. Cover bowl, stand in warm place about 45 minutes or until dough has doubled in size.

3. Turn dough onto floured surface, knead about 5 minutes or until smooth. Divide dough into 16 portions, knead into buns 15cm long. Place buns onto greased oven trays about 4cm apart, cover with lightly greased plastic wrap, stand in warm place about 10 minutes or until buns are well risen.

4. Remove plastic wrap. Bake buns in hot oven about 10 minutes. Lift buns onto wire rack, brush with glaze, cool. Spread evenly with warm icing, sprinkle with coconut.

5. Glaze: Combine all ingredients in small pan, stir over heat, without boiling, until gelatine is dissolved.

6. Icing: Sift icing sugar into small heatproof bowl, stir in butter and enough water to make a stiff paste; tint with colouring, if desired. Stir over hot water until spreadable.

Makes 16.

GREEK EASTER BREAD

2 teaspoons (7g) dry yeast
1 teaspoon caster sugar
3/4 cup (180ml) warm milk
1/2 cup (75g) plain flour
100g butter, melted
2 eggs, lightly beaten
1/3 cup (75g) caster sugar, extra
3 cups (450g) plain flour, extra
2 teaspoons ground aniseed
1/2 teaspoon salt
1 egg yolk
2 tablespoons milk, extra

1. Combine yeast, sugar and milk in large bowl, whisk until yeast is dissolved.

2. Whisk in sifted flour, cover, stand in warm place about 45 minutes or until mixture has doubled in size.

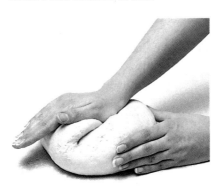

3. Whisk in butter, eggs and extra sugar. Stir in sifted extra flour, aniseed and salt in 2 batches. Turn dough onto floured surface, knead about 10 minutes or until smooth.

4. Place dough in large greased bowl, cover, stand in warm place about 1 1/2 hours or until dough has doubled in size. Turn dough onto floured surface, knead until smooth. Divide dough into 6 portions. Shape each portion into a 33cm sausage. Twist 2 sausages together; shape into a round. Repeat with remaining sausages. Place the 3 rounds close together on a lightly greased oven tray, brush joins with water, press rounds gently together.

5. Cover bread, stand in warm place about 45 minutes or until well risen. Brush bread with combined egg yolk and extra milk, bake in moderately hot oven 10 minutes, reduce heat to moderate, bake about a further 30 minutes.

2. Sift flour and salt into large bowl, rub in butter. Stir in yeast mixture, mix to a soft dough. Turn dough onto floured surface, knead about 5 minutes or until smooth and elastic. Place dough in large greased bowl, cover, stand in warm place about 1 hour or until dough has doubled in size.

3. Turn dough onto floured surface, knead until smooth, divide dough into 6 equal portions, knead into balls. Place baps about 5cm apart on floured oven tray. Dust lightly with a little extra sifted flour, cover with cloth. Stand in warm place about 10 minutes or until baps are well risen.

BAPS

2 teaspoons (7g) dry yeast
1 teaspoon sugar
½ cup (125ml) warm water
½ cup (125ml) warm milk
2¼ cups (335g) plain flour
1 teaspoon salt
40g butter

1. Combine yeast, sugar, water and milk in small bowl, whisk until yeast is dissolved. Cover bowl, stand in warm place about 10 minutes or until mixture is frothy.

4. Dust baps again with a little more sifted flour, indent centres with finger. Bake in hot oven about 15 minutes.
Makes 6.

ROTI

Dough can be made a day ahead and kept wrapped in refrigerator.

1 cup (150g) white plain flour
1 cup (160g) wholemeal plain flour
1 teaspoon salt
1 teaspoon ground coriander
½ teaspoon ground turmeric
2 teaspoons cumin seeds
1 tablespoon vegetable oil
¾ cup (180ml) water, approximately
90g ghee, approximately

1. Sift flours, salt and ground spices into large bowl. Make a well in flour, add seeds, oil and enough water to mix to a soft dough. Turn dough onto floured surface, knead 10 minutes. Wrap dough in plastic, refrigerate 30 minutes.

2. Divide dough into 16 portions, roll each portion on floured surface to 16cm round.

3. Heat heavy-based frying pan until very hot, add about 1 teaspoon of the ghee, quickly turn pan to coat base with ghee. Place roti into pan, cook about 1 minute or until roti is puffed slightly and bubbles begin to form. Turn roti, brown other side. Repeat with remaining ghee and dough. When ghee begins to burn in pan and a few roti have been cooked, wipe pan clean with absorbent paper.

Makes 16.

PARATHAS WITH SPICY POTATO FILLING

1 cup (160g) wholemeal plain flour
1 cup (150g) white plain flour
½ teaspoon salt
100g ghee, chopped
½ cup (125ml) water, approximately
100g ghee, extra

FILLING
1 large (300g) potato, chopped
½ small (125g) kumara, chopped
1 teaspoon coriander
    seeds, bruised
½ teaspoon ground cumin
¼ teaspoon cayenne pepper
¼ cup firmly packed fresh
    coriander leaves

4. Divide filling among 8 rounds. Spread filling over rounds, leaving 7mm borders. Brush borders with water, top with remaining rounds, press edges together to seal.

1. Sift flours and salt into large bowl, rub in ghee. Stir in enough water to make ingredients cling together.

5. Heat some of the extra ghee in large pan, add parathas in batches, cook until browned and slightly puffed on both sides; drain on absorbent paper. Repeat with remaining ghee and parathas.

2. Turn dough onto floured surface, knead about 10 minutes or until smooth.

6. Filling: Boil, steam or microwave potato and kumara until tender. Mash vegetables coarsely, stir in spices and coriander.

Makes 8.

3. Divide dough into 16 portions, roll each portion on floured surface into a 16cm round. Stack rounds between layers of plastic wrap to prevent drying out.

Pewter plate from Accoutrement; metal scoop from The Bay Tree Kitchen Shop; wire tray from Le Forge

PANETTONE

½ cup (85g) raisins
¼ cup (40g) mixed peel
½ cup (80g) sultanas
⅓ cup (80ml) marsala
8 teaspoons (28g) dry yeast
1 teaspoon caster sugar
¼ cup (60ml) warm milk
5 cups (750g) plain flour
1 teaspoon salt
¼ cup (55g) caster sugar, extra
3 eggs, lightly beaten
3 egg yolks
2 teaspoons grated orange rind
1 teaspoon vanilla essence
100g butter, softened
1 cup (250ml) warm milk, extra
1 egg, extra

1. Grease 2 x deep 20cm round cake pans. Using string, tie a collar of greased foil around outside of prepared pans, bringing foil about 6cm above rims.

2. Combine fruit with marsala in small bowl; cover, stand 30 minutes.

3. Combine yeast, sugar and milk in small bowl, whisk until yeast is dissolved. Cover, stand in warm place about 10 minutes or until mixture is frothy.

4. Sift flour, salt and extra sugar into large bowl, make well in centre, add eggs and egg yolks, then rind, essence, butter, extra milk, yeast mixture and undrained fruit mixture.

5. Beat dough vigorously with a wooden spoon for about 5 minutes. This beating is important. The dough will be soft like a cake batter, and will become elastic and leave the side of the bowl. Cover bowl with greased plastic wrap, stand in warm place about 30 minutes or until doubled in size. Remove plastic wrap.

6. Turn dough onto floured surface, knead until smooth. Cut dough in half, knead each half on a well-floured surface for about 5 minutes or until the dough loses its stickiness. Press dough into prepared pans. Cover, stand in warm place about 30 minutes or until doubled in size. Brush panettone with extra egg. Bake in moderately hot oven 15 minutes, reduce heat to moderate, bake about a further 30 minutes.

Makes 2.

PUMPERNICKEL BREAD

2 teaspoons (7g) dry yeast
1 teaspoon sugar
1 cup (250ml) warm water
50g butter, melted
1 tablespoon molasses
1 tablespoon caraway seeds
½ cup (85g) cornmeal
1½ cups (185g) rye flour
1 cup (150g) plain flour
2 tablespoons cocoa powder
1 teaspoon salt

1. Combine yeast, sugar and water in large bowl, whisk until yeast is dissolved; cover, stand in warm place about 10 minutes or until mixture is frothy.

2. Stir in butter and molasses, then seeds, cornmeal and sifted flours, cocoa and salt. Turn dough onto floured surface, knead about 10 minutes or until smooth.

3. Place dough into greased bowl, cover, stand in warm place about 2 hours or until dough has doubled in size.

4. Grease 8cm x 26cm bar pan, line sides of pan with 2 layers of baking paper, extending 5cm above edge of pan. Turn dough onto floured surface, knead until smooth. Press dough into prepared pan. Cover loosely, stand in warm place about 45 minutes or until dough has risen to top of pan.

5. Cover pan with a sheet of foil. Bake in moderate oven 15 minutes, remove foil, bake about a further 30 minutes.

BAGELS

3 teaspoons (10g) dry yeast
1 tablespoon caster sugar
½ cup (125ml) warm water
1 cup (250ml) warm milk
3 cups (450g) plain flour
3 teaspoons salt
1 tablespoon caster sugar, extra
1 egg yolk
1 teaspoon water, extra
1 tablespoon poppy seeds
2 teaspoons sea salt

1. Combine yeast, sugar, water and milk in large bowl, whisk until yeast is dissolved. Cover, stand in warm place about 10 minutes or until mixture is frothy.

2. Stir sifted flour, salt and extra sugar into yeast mixture in 2 batches; mix to a firm dough.

3. Turn dough onto floured surface, knead about 10 minutes or until dough is smooth and elastic. Place dough into large greased bowl, cover, stand in warm place about 1 hour or until dough has doubled in size.

4. Turn dough onto floured surface, knead until smooth; divide dough into 12 portions. Knead each portion into a ball. Press finger in centre of each ball to make a hole, rotate ball with finger until the hole is one-third of the size of the bagel. Place bagels about 3cm apart on greased oven trays, cover, stand in warm place about 15 minutes, or until risen.

5. Drop bagels individually into pan of boiling water; they must not touch. Turn bagels after 1 minute, boil further minute, remove with slotted spoon. Place bagels on greased oven trays. Brush tops with combined egg yolk and extra water, sprinkle with combined seeds and sea salt. Bake in moderately hot oven about 20 minutes. Cool on wire rack.

Makes 12.

STOLLEN

1¼ cups (310ml) milk
1 teaspoon salt
½ cup (110g) caster sugar
2 teaspoons (7g) dry yeast
1 cup (150g) plain flour
3 cups (450g) plain flour, extra
160g butter, melted
2 eggs, lightly beaten
1 tablespoon grated lemon rind
¼ cup (50g) glace cherries, chopped
¼ cup (40g) raisins, chopped
¼ cup (40g) mixed peel
2 rings (55g) glace pineapple, chopped
½ cup (80g) blanched almonds, chopped
½ teaspoon ground cinnamon
2 teaspoons caster sugar, extra
1 egg, lightly beaten, extra

1. Combine milk, salt and sugar in small pan, stir over heat until sugar is dissolved and milk warmed. Transfer to medium bowl.

2. Whisk in yeast and sifted flour, cover, stand in warm place about 10 minutes or until mixture is frothy.

3. Sift extra flour into large bowl. Stir in butter, eggs, rind, fruit, yeast mixture and nuts; mix to a soft dough.

4. Turn dough onto floured surface, knead about 5 minutes or until smooth and elastic. Halve dough, press each half into an 18cm x 25cm oval.

Sprinkle with combined cinnamon and extra sugar, fold dough almost in half. Place stollens onto greased oven trays, cover with greased plastic wrap. Stand in warm place about 40 minutes or until stollens are risen slightly.

Remove plastic wrap. Brush stollens with extra egg. Bake in moderately hot oven 10 minutes, reduce heat to moderate, bake about a further 15 minutes. Lift onto wire rack to cool.

Makes 2.

IRISH SODA BREAD

2²/₃ cups (420g) wholemeal
    plain flour
2¹/₂ cups (375g) white plain flour
1 teaspoon salt
1 teaspoon bicarbonate of soda
2³/₄ cups (680ml) buttermilk,
    approximately

1. Sift flours, salt and soda into large bowl. Stir in enough buttermilk to mix to a firm dough.

2. Turn dough onto floured surface, knead until just smooth. Shape dough into 20cm round, place on greased oven tray.

3. Cut 1cm deep slashes in bread in a cross, brush with a little milk. Bake in moderate oven about 50 minutes. Lift onto wire rack to cool.

ONION FOCACCIA

2 cups (300g) plain flour
½ teaspoon salt
2 teaspoons (7g) dry yeast
¼ cup (20g) grated parmesan
cheese
1 tablespoon chopped
fresh rosemary
1 tablespoon chopped fresh sage
2 teaspoons chopped fresh parsley
2 tablespoons olive oil
1 cup (250ml) warm water
1 small (80g) onion, finely sliced
1 tablespoon sea salt
1 tablespoon olive oil, extra

1. Sift flour and salt into large bowl, stir in yeast, cheese and herbs. Pour in oil and water, gradually stir in flour; mix to a soft dough.

2. Turn dough onto floured surface, knead about 5 minutes or until dough is smooth and elastic.

3. Place dough on greased oven tray, press into 24cm round. Cover dough with greased plastic wrap, stand in warm place about 1 hour or until doubled in size.

4. Remove plastic wrap. Sprinkle bread with onion and sea salt, drizzle with extra oil. Bake in hot oven about 25 minutes. Lift onto wire rack to cool.

CHELSEA BUNS

4 teaspoons (14g) dry yeast
1 teaspoon caster sugar
3¾ cups (560g) plain flour
1½ cups (375ml) warm milk
½ teaspoon ground cinnamon
¼ teaspoon ground nutmeg
½ teaspoon mixed spice
2 teaspoons grated orange rind
1 tablespoon caster sugar, extra
1 egg, lightly beaten
45g butter, melted
15g butter, melted, extra
2 tablespoons raspberry jam
½ cup (75g) dried currants
¼ cup (50g) brown sugar
½ cup (60g) chopped pecans,
**   toasted**
3 teaspoons honey

COFFEE ICING
1½ cups (240g) icing sugar mixture
15g butter, melted
2 tablespoons warm milk
3 teaspoons coffee powder

1. Combine yeast, caster sugar, 1 tablespoon of the flour and milk in small bowl, whisk until yeast is dissolved. Cover, stand in warm place about 10 minutes or until mixture is frothy.

2. Combine remaining sifted flour, spices, rind and extra caster sugar in large bowl, stir in egg, butter and yeast mixture; mix to a soft dough.

3. Turn dough onto floured surface, knead about 10 minutes or until smooth and elastic. Place dough in large greased bowl, cover, stand in warm place about 1 hour or until doubled in size.

4. Turn dough onto floured surface, knead 1 minute. Roll dough into a 23cm x 36cm rectangle. Brush dough with extra butter, spread with jam. Sprinkle with combined currants, brown sugar and nuts, leaving a 2cm border.

5. Roll dough up from long side, like a Swiss roll. Cut into 12 slices. Place slices cut side up in 2 greased deep 22cm round cake pans. Cover, stand in warm place about 30 minutes or until buns have risen slightly.

Bake in moderately hot oven about 30 minutes. Cool buns in pan 10 minutes, transfer to wire rack. Brush hot buns with honey, drizzle with coffee icing.

6. Coffee Icing: Sift icing sugar into small bowl, stir in butter, milk and coffee, stir until smooth.

Makes 2.

PITA BREAD

2 teaspoons (7g) dry yeast
1 teaspoon sugar
1¼ cups (310ml) warm milk
4¼ cups (635g) plain flour
1 teaspoon salt
½ cup (125ml) plain yogurt
1 egg, lightly beaten
¼ cup (60ml) water
1 tablespoon olive oil

3. Turn dough onto floured surface, knead until smooth. Divide dough into 8 equal portions. Knead each portion into a ball, place onto lightly floured oven tray, cover, stand in warm place about 30 minutes or until doubled in size.

1. Combine yeast, sugar and milk in small bowl, whisk until yeast is dissolved. Cover, stand in warm place about 10 minutes or until mixture is frothy.

2. Sift flour and salt into large bowl. Stir in yeast mixture and combined yogurt, egg, water and oil, mix to a soft dough. Turn dough onto floured surface, knead about 10 minutes or until smooth and elastic. Place dough in greased bowl, cover, stand in warm place about 1 hour or until doubled in size.

4. Preheat oven to highest temperature. Roll each ball into a 25cm round. Heat an oven tray in a very hot oven, place 1 round at a time onto tray, bake in very hot oven, on top shelf, for about 5 minutes or until bread is lightly browned and rounds begin to expand. Wrap cooked pita bread in a cloth to keep warm before serving.

Makes 8.

DAMPER

3½ cups (525g) self-raising flour
1 teaspoon salt
2 teaspoons caster sugar
40g butter
½ cup (125ml) milk
1¼ cups (310ml) water,
 approximately

1. Sift flour, salt and sugar into large bowl, rub in butter. Stir in milk and enough water to mix to a sticky dough.

2. Turn dough onto floured surface, knead until just smooth. Place dough on greased oven tray, press into 16cm round.

3. Cut a cross in the dough, about 1cm deep. Brush dough with a little extra milk, then sprinkle with a little extra flour. Bake in moderately hot oven about 45 minutes. Lift onto wire rack to cool.

Scones

Rise to the occasion with our easy-to-follow basic scone method, and you will soon see there's no mystery involved in making good scones. All these recipes have the same simple style so you can progress to some delicious new combinations and choices. Scones are best made close to serving.

1. MAKE A SOFT, STICKY DOUGH

Most recipes give an approximate amount of liquid. This allows for the rate at which the flour absorbs liquid. The moisture content of the flour varies, depending on the flour's freshness and the weather. The dough must be soft and sticky and just hold its shape when turned out.

2. USE MINIMUM FLOUR WHILE HANDLING DOUGH

Turn dough onto lightly floured surface, dust your hands with flour and shape the dough into a smooth ball by working the dough gently into a manageable, smooth shape. This will give you smooth-topped scones. Avoid excess flour, which upsets the ingredients' balance and interferes with browning. Flatten the dough gently with your hand until it is an even thickness all over, press from the centre outwards. Use a floured, sharp metal cutter to cut as many scones as possible from the dough; these scones will be the lightest. Lightly knead the scraps together. Press dough out again slightly thicker to help make up for the second handling.

3. BAKE AT HIGH TEMPERATURES

The oven temperature should be hot to very hot for good scones. They need to rise quickly to be light. Ovens vary greatly; always be guided by your own oven manufacturer's instructions for oven positions and temperatures. Usually, one test batch of scones in your oven will give you confidence to adjust time, temperature and oven positions. We prefer to cook scones close together in lightly greased, shallow aluminium cake pans. This method will give you straight scones with crusty tops and bottoms and soft sides. They need to be cooked slightly longer than scones on oven trays. If you prefer, cook scones on lightly greased oven trays, but only grease where the scones sit. If you like a scone crusty all over, space the scones about 1cm apart on the tray. If you like crusty tops and bottoms, place the scones just touching each other on the tray. They will support each other as they rise, but almost always some or all of the outside scones will topple and/or overcook.

■ Recipes are not suitable to microwave.

COOLING SCONES

▓ Always turn scones out of the pans or slide off oven trays onto wire racks. If you prefer crusty scones, cool the scones uncovered. To soften the crust, wrap hot scones in a clean tea-towel.

GLAZING

▓ Glazing removes excess flour from the tops of scones and encourages them to brown. We use a brush dipped in water, milk or egg. Water results in a light brown, egg a golden brown, and milk is a good compromise. Glazing is not necessary.

FREEZING

▓ To freeze uncooked scones: Leave scones in pan or freeze individually on oven tray, then place in freezer bags; press to expel air or use a freezer pump. It is important that they be airtight. Correctly wrapped uncooked scones can be frozen for up to 2 months.

▓ To freeze cooked scones: Place cold scones in freezer bags, press to expel air or use a freezer pump. It is important that they be airtight. Correctly wrapped cooked scones can be frozen for up to 2 months.

▓ To bake uncooked frozen scones: Remove from freezer bag, bake frozen scones in hot oven for 20 minutes.

▓ To reheat cooked frozen scones: Remove from freezer bag, then wrap unthawed scones in single layer tightly in foil. Reheat in moderate oven for about 20 minutes.

TO TEST SCONES ARE COOKED

▓ Scones should be browned and sound hollow when tapped firmly on the top. The scones in the middle are the ones to tap; they will take the longest to cook.

Clockwise from back: Basic Scones; Lemon and Currant; Apricot Wholemeal; Cumin Seed and Oregano (recipes over page).

BASIC SCONES

2½ cups (375g) self-raising flour
1 tablespoon caster sugar
¼ teaspoon salt
30g butter
¾ cup (180ml) milk
½ cup (125ml) water, approximately

1. Grease a 23cm square slab cake pan. Sift flour, sugar and salt into large bowl, rub in butter with fingertips.

2. Use a knife to stir in milk and enough water to mix to a soft, sticky dough.

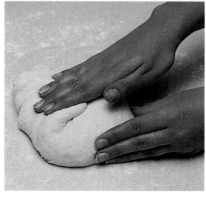

3. Turn dough onto lightly floured surface, knead quickly and lightly until dough is smooth.

4. Use hand to press dough out evenly to 2cm thickness, cut into 5cm rounds. Gently knead scraps of dough together, and repeat pressing and cutting out of dough. Place scones in prepared pan; brush with a little extra milk, if desired. Bake in very hot oven about 15 minutes. Makes 16.

VARIATIONS

LEMON AND CURRANT

1 quantity basic scone ingredients
½ cup (75g) dried currants
2 teaspoons grated lemon rind

Add currants and rind to flour mixture. Proceed as for basic scone method.

APRICOT WHOLEMEAL

½ cup (75g) chopped dried apricots
½ cup (125ml) boiling water
1½ cups (225g) white
  self-raising flour
1 cup (160g) wholemeal
  self-raising flour
1 tablespoon caster sugar
¼ teaspoon salt
30g butter
¾ cup (180ml) milk, approximately

Place apricots in small heatproof bowl, pour over boiling water, stand 15 minutes or until cool. Proceed as for basic scone method. Add undrained apricot mixture after butter is rubbed into the flour, and enough milk to mix to a soft, sticky dough.

CUMIN SEED AND OREGANO

2 tablespoons chopped
  fresh oregano
3 teaspoons cumin seeds
2 teaspoons ground cumin
1 quantity basic scone ingredients
1 tablespoon tomato paste

Add oregano, seeds and cumin to flour mixture. Proceed as for basic scone method, combining paste with milk.

RHUBARB GINGER DAMPER

15g butter
3 stems (200g) rhubarb,
  finely chopped
2 cups (300g) self-raising flour
pinch bicarbonate of soda
teaspoon ground cinnamon
1/2 cup (60g) ground almonds
2 tablespoons finely chopped
  crystallised ginger
1/3 cup (75g) caster sugar
1 cup (250ml) milk, approximately
2 tablespoons caster sugar, extra

Melt butter in small pan, add rhubarb, cook, stirring, about 5 minutes or until rhubarb is just tender; cool. Sift flour, soda and cinnamon into medium bowl, stir in nuts, ginger, sugar and rhubarb. Stir in enough milk to mix to a soft, sticky dough. Turn dough onto floured surface, knead until smooth. Divide dough in half, place halves onto greased oven trays, shape into 15cm rounds. Mark rounds into 8 wedges, sprinkle with extra sugar. Bake in hot oven about 20 minutes.

Makes 2.

ABOVE: Rhubarb Ginger Damper.

99

ZUCCHINI GEMS WITH ORANGE HONEY BUTTER

Heat ungreased gem irons in hot oven for 5 minutes just before use; grease with cooking oil spray.

30g butter
2/3 cup (150g) caster sugar
1 egg
1 small (90g) zucchini, finely grated
2 tablespoons dried currants
1 1/4 cups (185g) self-raising flour
pinch ground nutmeg
1/2 teaspoon ground cinnamon
1/4 cup (60ml) milk

ORANGE HONEY BUTTER
100g butter, softened
2 tablespoons grated orange rind
2 tablespoons orange marmalade
1/2 teaspoon mixed spice
2 tablespoons honey

Beat butter, sugar and egg in small bowl with electric mixer until just combined. Stir in zucchini and currants, then sifted flour and spices with milk in 2 batches. Drop tablespoons of mixture into hot gem irons. Bake in hot oven about 10 minutes. Turn onto wire rack. Serve warm gems with orange honey butter.

Orange Honey Butter: Beat butter and rind in small bowl with electric mixer until smooth; stir in remaining ingredients.

Makes 24.

ABOVE: Zucchini Gems with Orange Honey Butter.
RIGHT: Caramel Apple Pull-Apart.

CARAMEL APPLE PULL-APART

2 cups (300g) self-raising flour
30g butter
1 cup (250ml) milk, approximately
1/3 cup (65g) firmly packed
   brown sugar
410g can pie apples
pinch ground nutmeg
1/2 teaspoon ground cinnamon
1/4 cup (30g) chopped pecans, toasted

CARAMEL
1/4 cup (60ml) cream
20g butter
1/2 cup (100g) firmly packed
   brown sugar

Grease deep 22cm round cake pan. Sift flour into medium bowl, rub in butter, stir in enough milk to mix to a soft, sticky dough. Turn dough onto floured surface, knead until smooth. Roll dough on floured baking paper to 21cm x 40cm rectangle. Sprinkle dough with sugar, spread with combined apples and spices to within 3cm from long edge. Using paper as a guide, roll dough up like a Swiss roll.

Use a floured, serrated knife to cut roll into 12 slices. Place 11 slices upright around edge of pan; place remaining slice in centre. Bake pull-apart in moderately hot oven about 25 minutes. Stand a few minutes before turning onto wire rack to cool. Brush hot pull-apart evenly with caramel, sprinkle with nuts.

Caramel: Combine all ingredients in small pan, stir constantly over heat, without boiling, until sugar is dissolved. Simmer uncovered, without stirring, about 3 minutes or until mixture is thickened slightly.

Setting from Opus Design

Jam pot from Ventura Design

BUTTERMILK SCONES

3 cups (450g) self-raising flour
1/4 teaspoon salt
1 teaspoon icing sugar mixture
60g butter
1 3/4 cups (430ml) buttermilk,
  approximately

Grease 23cm square slab cake pan. Sift dry ingredients into large bowl, rub in butter, stir in enough buttermilk to mix to a soft, sticky dough. Turn dough onto floured surface, knead until smooth. Press dough out to 2cm thickness, cut into 5.5cm rounds. Place scones into prepared pan. Bake in very hot oven about 15 minutes.

Makes 16.

BACON, EGG AND MUSTARD SCONES

2 bacon rashers, finely chopped
2 1/4 cups (335g) self-raising flour
90g butter, chopped
2 hard-boiled eggs, finely chopped
1/4 cup (20g) finely grated
  parmesan cheese
2 tablespoons chopped
  fresh chives
1 tablespoon seeded mustard
1 cup (250ml) milk, approximately
2 tablespoons finely grated
  parmesan cheese, extra

Grease 23cm round sandwich cake pan. Cook bacon in pan, stirring, until crisp; drain, cool. Sift flour into medium bowl, rub in butter. Add bacon, eggs, cheese, chives and mustard, stir in enough milk to mix to a soft, sticky dough. Turn dough onto floured surface, knead until smooth. Press dough out to 2cm thickness, cut into 5cm rounds. Place scones into prepared pan, brush with a little extra milk, sprinkle with extra cheese. Bake in very hot oven about 15 minutes.

Makes 16.

ABOVE: Buttermilk Scones.
RIGHT: Bacon, Egg and Mustard Scones.

SPICY FRUIT SCONES

1¼ cups (310ml) hot strong
   strained black tea
¾ cup (135g) mixed dried fruit
3 cups (450g) self-raising flour
1 teaspoon ground cinnamon
1 teaspoon mixed spice
2 tablespoons caster sugar
20g butter
½ cup (125ml) sour cream,
   approximately

Grease 23cm square slab cake pan. Combine tea and fruit in small heat-proof bowl, cover, stand 20 minutes or until mixture is cold. Sift dry ingredients into large bowl, rub in butter. Stir in fruit mixture and enough sour cream to mix to a soft, sticky dough. Turn dough onto floured surface, knead until smooth. Press dough out to 2cm thickness. Cut into 5.5cm rounds. Place scones into prepared pan. Bake in hot oven about 15 minutes.

Makes 16.

ABOVE: Spicy Fruit Scones.
RIGHT: Fig and Apple Turnover.

FIG AND APPLE TURNOVER

3/4 cup (135g) roughly chopped dried figs
1/4 cup (60ml) boiling water
2 cups (300g) self-raising flour
1 tablespoon caster sugar
30g butter
1 cup (250ml) milk, approximately
1 large (200g) apple, peeled, quartered
2 teaspoons caster sugar, extra

Combine figs and water in small heat-proof bowl, cover, stand 10 minutes. Process undrained fig mixture until smooth. Sift flour and sugar into medium bowl, rub in butter, stir in enough milk to mix to a soft, sticky dough. Turn dough onto floured surface, knead until smooth. Roll dough to 23cm x 30cm oval; spread with fig mixture.

Slice apple quarters thinly with a vegetable peeler; place over half the dough lengthways, sprinkle with extra sugar. Fold dough over lengthways to cover about two-thirds of the apple. Transfer to greased oven tray; shape dough into an oval, cut diagonal slashes about 3cm apart on top of turnover, brush with a little milk. Bake in very hot oven about 15 minutes. Serve dusted with icing sugar, if desired.

APRICOT CREAM CHEESE RING

1/3 cup (50g) finely chopped
  dried apricots
1/2 cup (125ml) apricot jam
1/3 cup (45g) slivered almonds,
  roughly chopped, toasted
2 cups (300g) self-raising flour
30g butter
125g packet cream
  cheese, chopped
1/4 cup (55g) caster sugar
1/2 cup (60g) ground almonds
1/2 cup (125ml) milk, approximately
2 tablespoons flaked almonds,
  toasted

GLAZE
15g butter
1 teaspoon grated lemon rind
2 teaspoons lemon juice
1/2 cup (80g) icing sugar mixture

Cover apricots with boiling water in heatproof bowl, cover, stand 5 minutes. Drain apricots, combine apricots in bowl with jam and slivered almonds.

Process flour, butter and cheese until fine. Transfer mixture to large bowl, stir in sugar and ground almonds, then enough milk to mix to a soft, sticky dough. Turn dough onto floured surface, knead until smooth. Roll dough on floured baking paper to 28cm x 40cm rectangle, spread with apricot mixture to within 2cm of 1 long edge.

Using paper as a guide, roll up from long side without border, like a Swiss roll, place on greased oven tray, shape into a round, press ends together to form a neat round. Use floured, serrated knife to cut roll at about 3cm intervals to within about 2cm of inside circle. Bake in moderately hot oven about 30 minutes. Transfer to serving plate, brush with glaze, sprinkle with flaked almonds.

Glaze: Melt butter in small pan, stir in remaining ingredients.

RIGHT: Carrot Banana Scones.
BELOW RIGHT: Golden Honey Muesli Scones.
BELOW: Apricot Cream Cheese Ring.

CARROT BANANA SCONES

You will need 1 large (230g) over-ripe banana and 1 medium (120g) carrot for this recipe.

**2 cups (300g) white
  self-raising flour**
**1/2 cup (80g) wholemeal
  self-raising flour**
1/2 teaspoon ground cardamom
40g butter
**1/3 cup (65g) firmly packed
  brown sugar**
1/2 cup mashed banana
1/3 cup finely grated carrot
1/4 cup (30g) finely chopped walnuts
1/4 cup (40g) finely chopped raisins
3/4 cup (180ml) milk, approximately

ORANGE CREAM
**50g packaged cream cheese,
  chopped**
50g butter, chopped
1/2 teaspoon grated orange rind
1/2 cup (80g) icing sugar mixture

Grease 23cm round sandwich cake pan. Sift flours and cardamom into large bowl, rub in butter, add sugar, banana, carrot, nuts and raisins, stir in enough milk to mix to a soft, sticky dough. Turn dough onto floured surface, knead until smooth. Press dough out to 2cm thickness, cut into 5.5cm rounds, place into prepared pan. Bake in very hot oven about 20 minutes. Serve with orange cream.

Orange Cream: Beat cheese, butter and rind in small bowl with electric mixer until as white as possible. Gradually beat in sifted icing sugar.

Makes 12.

GOLDEN HONEY
MUESLI SCONES

2 cups (300g) self-raising flour
1 teaspoon ground cinnamon
20g butter
1/2 cup (65g) toasted muesli
1/4 cup (60ml) honey
3/4 cup (180ml) milk, approximately
1 tablespoon demerara sugar

Grease 20cm round sandwich cake pan. Sift flour and cinnamon into medium bowl, rub in butter, stir in muesli. Add honey, stir in enough milk to mix to a soft, sticky dough. Turn dough onto floured surface, knead until smooth.

Press dough out to 2cm thickness, cut into 5.5cm rounds. Place scones into prepared pan, brush with a little extra milk, sprinkle with sugar. Bake in very hot oven about 15 minutes.

Makes 12.

Setting from Opus Design

HONEY WHOLEMEAL SCONES

**2 cups (300g) white
self-raising flour
1 cup (160g) wholemeal
self-raising flour
1/2 teaspoon ground cinnamon
20g butter
1/4 cup (60ml) honey
1 cup (250ml) milk, approximately**

Grease 19cm x 29cm rectangular slice pan. Sift dry ingredients into medium bowl, rub in butter, stir in honey and enough milk to mix to a soft, sticky dough. Turn dough onto floured surface, knead until smooth. Press dough out to 2cm thickness. Cut into 5.5cm rounds. Place scones into prepared pan. Bake in hot oven about 20 minutes.

Makes 15.

SMOKED SALMON AND SOUR CREAM SCONES

**2 cups (300g) self-raising flour
150g smoked salmon, chopped
1/3 cup chopped fresh dill tips
1/4 teaspoon ground black pepper
1/3 cup (80ml) sour cream
1 cup (250ml) buttermilk,
approximately**

DILL CREAM
**1/2 cup (125ml) sour cream
1/4 cup chopped fresh dill tips**

Grease 19cm x 29cm rectangular slice pan. Sift flour into medium bowl, stir in salmon, dill and pepper, then sour cream and enough buttermilk to mix to a soft, sticky dough.

Turn dough onto floured surface, knead until smooth, press dough out to 2cm thickness, cut into 5.5cm rounds. Place scones into prepared pan. Bake

in very hot oven about 15 minutes. Serve with dill cream.

Dill Cream: Combine ingredients in small bowl; mix well.

Makes 12.

ABOVE: Smoked Salmon and Sour Cream Scones.
RIGHT: Honey Wholemeal Scones.

Coffee cup and butter tray from Ventura Design

PISTACHIO LIME SYRUP GEMS

Heat ungreased gem irons in hot oven for 5 minutes just before use; grease with cooking oil spray.

30g butter
1 teaspoon grated lime rind
1/3 cup (75g) caster sugar
1 egg
1 1/4 cups (185g) self-raising flour
2/3 cup (160ml) milk
**1/4 cup (35g) finely chopped
    pistachios**

LIME SYRUP
2 tablespoons lime juice
2 tablespoons water
1/3 cup (75g) caster sugar

Beat butter, rind, sugar and egg in small bowl with electric mixer until combined. Stir in sifted flour and milk in 2 batches. Drop tablespoons of mixture into prepared gem irons, sprinkle with nuts. Bake in moderately hot oven about 12 minutes. Turn onto wire rack, brush all over with hot lime syrup.
Lime Syrup: Combine all ingredients in small pan, stir over heat, without boiling, until sugar is dissolved, simmer, uncovered, without stirring, 2 minutes.
Makes 24.

CHEESY CORIANDER PESTO KNOTS

2¼ cups (335g) self-raising flour
2 teaspoons caster sugar
¼ teaspoon salt
30g butter
1 cup (250ml) milk, approximately
100g hard goats' cheese
ground black pepper

PESTO
⅔ cup firmly packed fresh
    coriander leaves and stems
½ cup (40g) coarsely grated
    parmesan cheese
½ cup (80g) pine nuts, toasted
1 clove garlic, crushed
2 tablespoons olive oil
1 tablespoon water

Sift flour, sugar and salt into medium bowl, rub in butter. Stir in enough milk to mix to a soft, sticky dough. Turn dough onto floured surface, knead until smooth. Roll dough to 17cm x 30cm rectangle. Spread dough with pesto, top with crumbled cheese; sprinkle with pepper.

Cut dough crossways into 3cm strips. Hold both ends of a dough strip in each hand, loop dough as if to make a knot; tuck ends under neatly. Place knots on greased oven trays about 2cm apart. Bake in very hot oven about 15 minutes.

Pesto: Process coriander, cheese, nuts and garlic until combined. With motor operating, add oil in a thin stream; add water, process until smooth.

Makes 10.

GOLDEN PUMPKIN SCONES

You will need to cook about 400g pumpkin for this recipe.

60g butter
¼ cup (55g) caster sugar
1 egg
2 tablespoons golden syrup
1 cup cooked mashed pumpkin
2⅔ cups (400g) self-raising flour
½ teaspoon ground nutmeg
⅓ cup (80ml) milk, approximately

Grease 23cm round sandwich cake pan. Beat butter and sugar in small bowl with electric mixer until combined, gradually beat in egg and golden syrup; transfer to large bowl. Stir in pumpkin and half the sifted dry ingredients, then remaining dry ingredients with enough milk to mix to a soft, sticky dough.

Turn dough onto floured surface, knead until smooth. Press dough out to 2cm thickness, cut into 5.5cm rounds. Place scones into prepared pan. Bake in very hot oven about 20 minutes.

Makes 12.

Bowl and tea-towel from Opus Design

LEFT: Pistachio Lime Syrup Gems.
TOP LEFT: Cheesy Coriander Pesto Knots.
ABOVE: Golden Pumpkin Scones.

GLAZED APRICOT ALMOND SCONES

3 cups (450g) self-raising flour
1 teaspoon mixed spice
2 teaspoons caster sugar
30g butter
1 cup (150g) dried apricots,
   chopped
1/3 cup (45g) slivered almonds,
   toasted, roughly chopped
1 egg, lightly beaten
1 1/4 cups (310ml) milk,
   approximately
2 tablespoons sieved apricot jam

Grease 23cm square slab pan. Sift
flour, spice and sugar into large bowl,
rub in butter. Add apricots and nuts, stir
in egg and enough milk to mix to a soft,
sticky dough.

   Turn dough onto floured surface,
knead until smooth. Press dough out to
3cm thickness, cut into 5.5cm rounds.
Place scones into prepared pan. Bake
in hot oven about 15 minutes, brush
with jam.

Makes 16.

FRUIT AND NUT SCROLLS

*If you prefer, you can use
1¼ cups (380g) bottled fruit
mince in this recipe.*

3 cups (450g) self-raising flour
2 teaspoons caster sugar
50g butter
**1⅓ cups (330ml) buttermilk,
   approximately**

FILLING
¼ cup (40g) sultanas
¼ cup (35g) dried currants
¼ cup (35g) chopped dried apricots
**¼ cup (50g) chopped
   seeded prunes**
**1 medium (150g) apple, peeled,
   finely chopped**
2 tablespoons flaked almonds
2 teaspoons grated orange rind
2 tablespoons orange juice
½ teaspoon ground cloves
2 teaspoons rum or brandy
¼ cup (50g) brown sugar

APRICOT GLAZE
2 tablespoons apricot jam
2 teaspoons water

ICING
⅓ cup (55g) icing sugar mixture
1 teaspoon hot water

Sift flour and sugar into large bowl, rub
in butter. Stir in enough buttermilk to
mix to a soft, sticky dough. Turn dough
onto floured surface, knead until
smooth. Roll dough to 26cm x 36cm
rectangle, spread with filling. Roll
dough firmly from long side, like a
Swiss roll. Cut roll into 2cm slices,
place slices cut-side-up 3cm apart onto
greased oven trays. Bake in very hot
oven about 15 minutes. Brush with hot
apricot glaze, drizzle with icing.
Filling: Combine all ingredients in
medium bowl; mix well.
Apricot Glaze: Combine jam and
water in small pan, simmer few minutes
or until glaze thickens slightly; strain.
Icing: Combine icing sugar and water
in small bowl, stir until smooth, pipe or
drizzle over scrolls.
Makes 18.

Coffee cup and butter tray from Ventura Design

BLUEBERRY GINGER SCONES WITH CUSTARD CREAM

2 cups (300g) self-raising flour
3 teaspoons ground ginger
¼ cup (55g) caster sugar
50g butter
**½ cup (75g) fresh or frozen
   blueberries**
¼ cup (60ml) sour cream
½ cup (125ml) milk, approximately

CUSTARD CREAM
1 cup (250ml) thickened cream
½ cup (125ml) thick custard
2 tablespoons icing sugar mixture

Grease 20cm round sandwich cake
pan. Sift flour, ginger and sugar into
medium bowl, rub in butter, add berries
and sour cream. Stir in enough milk to
mix to a soft, sticky dough. Turn dough
onto floured surface, knead until
smooth. Press dough out to 2cm thickness, cut into 5cm rounds. Place
scones into prepared pan. Bake in very
hot oven about 15 minutes. Serve
scones with custard cream, dusted with
sifted icing sugar, if desired.
Custard Cream: Beat cream, custard
and sugar in small bowl with electric
mixer until soft peaks form.

Makes 12.

*LEFT: Glazed Apricot Almond Scones.
TOP LEFT: Fruit and Nut Scrolls.
RIGHT: Blueberry Ginger Scones with
Custard Cream.*

SAGE PASTRAMI SCONES

**1½ cups (225g) white
    self-raising flour**
**½ cup (80g) wholemeal
    self-raising flour**
15g butter
2 tablespoons chopped fresh sage
60g pastrami, chopped
1 cup (250ml) milk, approximately

Grease 20cm round sandwich cake pan. Sift flours into medium bowl, rub in butter; stir in sage and pastrami. Stir in enough milk to mix to a soft, sticky dough. Turn dough onto floured surface, knead until smooth. Press dough out to 2cm thickness, cut into 5cm rounds. Place scones into prepared pan. Bake in hot oven about 20 minutes.

Makes 12.

CHOC FLORENTINE SCONES

2 cups (300g) self-raising flour
¼ cup (25g) cocoa powder
2 tablespoons caster sugar
1 teaspoon ground cinnamon
30g butter
**¼ cup (40g) blanched almonds,
    toasted, finely chopped**
**¼ cup (60g) chopped red
    glace cherries**
¼ cup (60g) chopped glace apricots
**¼ cup (55g) chopped glace
    pineapple**
1 cup (250ml) milk, approximately
150g dark chocolate, melted

Grease 20cm round sandwich cake pan. Sift flour, cocoa, sugar and cinnamon into medium bowl; rub in butter. Stir in nuts and fruit. Stir in enough milk to mix to a soft, sticky dough. Turn dough onto floured surface, knead until combined. Press dough out to 2.5cm thickness, cut into 5.5cm rounds. Place scones into prepared pan. Bake in hot oven about 25 minutes. Turn scones onto wire rack to cool. Spread tops of scones with chocolate, swirl with fork when almost set.

Makes 12.

ABOVE: Sage Pastrami Scones.
RIGHT: Choc Florentine Scones.

Coffee pot and cup from Ventura Design

Mustard Jar from The Bay Tree Kitchen Shop

CRUSTY CHEESE AND MUSTARD DAMPERETTES

4 cups (600g) self-raising flour
1 teaspoon dry mustard
30g butter
2 cups (500ml) milk, approximately

TOPPING
30g butter
2 tablespoons seeded mustard
1/2 teaspoon cayenne pepper
1 1/2 cups (120g) coarsely grated
fresh parmesan cheese

Sift flour and mustard into large bowl, rub in butter. Stir in enough milk to mix to a soft, sticky dough. Turn dough onto floured surface, knead until smooth. Press dough out to about 1.5cm thickness; cut into 7cm rounds. Place rounds, just touching, on greased oven trays; sprinkle with topping. Bake in hot oven about 15 minutes.
Topping: Melt butter in small pan, remove from heat, stir in remaining ingredients.
Makes 14.

FARMHOUSE SPINACH AND DOUBLE CHEESE PLAIT

1 bunch (500g) English spinach
15g butter
1 medium (350g) leek,
finely chopped
2 teaspoons chopped fresh thyme
2 cups (300g) self-raising flour
1 cup (80g) finely grated fresh
parmesan cheese
1 teaspoon seasoned pepper
1/4 cup chopped fresh basil
3/4 cup (150g) feta cheese, crumbled
1 cup (250ml) milk, approximately

Add spinach to pan of boiling water, boil 1 minute, drain, rinse under cold water; drain well. Squeeze excess moisture from spinach, chop finely. Heat butter in pan, add leek and thyme, cook, stirring occasionally, until leek is soft. Add spinach, cook, stirring, about 5 minutes or until any liquid has evaporated; cool.

Sift flour into medium bowl, stir in parmesan, pepper, basil, three-quarters of the feta cheese, spinach mixture and enough milk to mix to a soft, sticky dough. Turn dough onto floured surface, knead until smooth. Divide dough into 3 pieces, shape into 36cm sausages. Plait sausages together on greased oven tray, sprinkle with remaining feta cheese. Bake in moderately hot oven about 40 minutes.

LEFT: Crusty Cheese and Mustard Damperettes.
ABOVE: Farmhouse Spinach and Double Cheese Plait.

Yellow tray and glasses from Ventura Design

KUMARA AND GRUYERE WEDGES

You will need to cook about 300g kumara for this recipe.

350g gruyere cheese
2½ cups (375g) self-raising flour
40g butter
¼ cup chopped fresh chives
1 egg, lightly beaten
¾ cup cooked mashed kumara
½ cup (125ml) milk, approximately
1 egg, lightly beaten, extra

SPICY TOPPING
2 teaspoons coriander seeds,
** lightly crushed**
2 teaspoons cumin seeds
½ teaspoon crushed dried chilli
2 tablespoons finely chopped
** unsalted roasted cashews**

Grease deep 19cm square cake pan. Cut cheese into 1cm cubes.

Sift flour into large bowl, rub in butter; stir in cheese and chives. Add egg and kumara, stir in enough milk to mix to a soft, sticky dough. Turn dough onto floured surface, knead until smooth. Press dough into prepared pan, brush with extra egg, sprinkle with spicy topping; press topping firmly onto dough.

Using a floured, serrated knife, cut dough into quarters, then diagonally into 16 triangles. Bake in very hot oven 15 minutes, reduce heat to moderately hot, bake about further 15 minutes. Stand a few minutes before turning onto wire rack to cool.

Spicy Topping: Combine all ingredients in small bowl; mix well.

Makes 16.

CARDAMOM MARMALADE SCONES

2¹/₂ cups (375g) self-raising flour
1 teaspoon ground cardamom
30g butter
2 teaspoons grated orange rind
1 tablespoon caster sugar
¹/₃ cup (80ml) orange marmalade
1 cup (250ml) milk, approximately

MARMALADE BUTTER
125g butter
1 tablespoon orange marmalade

Grease 23cm square slab cake pan. Sift flour and cardamom into large bowl, rub in butter. Add rind, sugar and marmalade, stir in enough milk to mix to a soft, sticky dough. Turn dough onto floured surface, knead until smooth. Press dough out to 2cm thickness, cut into 5cm rounds. Place scones into prepared pan. Bake in hot oven about 15 minutes. Serve with marmalade butter.

Marmalade Butter: Beat butter in small bowl with electric mixer until as white as possible; stir in marmalade.

Makes 16.

PEPPERY LOTS-OF-SEED SCONES

2 cups (300g) self-raising flour
30g butter
2 tablespoons poppy seeds
2 tablespoons sesame seeds
2 tablespoons sunflower
seed kernels
2 tablespoons pumpkin seed
kernels, chopped
1 tablespoon chopped fresh
rosemary
1 teaspoon cracked black pepper
¹/₂ cup (60g) grated smoked cheese
1 egg, lightly beaten
1 cup (250ml) milk, approximately
1 tablespoon sesame seeds, extra

Grease 19cm x 29cm rectangular slice pan. Sift flour into medium bowl, rub in butter, add seeds, kernels, rosemary, pepper and cheese. Stir in egg and enough milk to mix to a soft, sticky dough, turn dough onto floured surface, knead until smooth. Press dough out to 3cm thickness, cut into 5.5cm rounds, place rounds into prepared pan, brush with a little extra milk, sprinkle with extra seeds. Bake in hot oven about 15 minutes.

Makes 12.

LEFT: Kumara and Gruyere Wedges.
ABOVE: Cardamom Marmalade Scones.
RIGHT: Peppery Lots-of-Seed Scones.

PIZZA BUNS

2 cups (300g) self-raising flour
15g butter
3/4 cup (180ml) milk, approximately
1 tablespoon chopped fresh thyme
2 teaspoons packaged
breadcrumbs

FILLING
1 tablespoon olive oil
1/2 small (40g) onion, finely chopped
3 bacon rashers, finely chopped
1 clove garlic, crushed
60g mushrooms, finely chopped
3 seeded black olives,
finely chopped
1 tablespoon tomato paste
1 tablespoon chopped fresh thyme

Grease 20cm ring cake pan. Sift flour into medium bowl, rub in butter, stir in enough milk to mix to a soft, sticky dough. Turn dough onto floured surface, knead until smooth. Divide dough into 8 pieces, knead each piece until smooth, press each piece to 10cm round, fill with a tablespoon of filling, pinch edges together to seal, shape into balls. Place balls into prepared pan. Brush with remaining oil, sprinkle with combined thyme and breadcrumbs. Bake in very hot oven 10 minutes, reduce heat to moderately hot, bake about further 20 minutes.
Filling: Heat half the oil in pan, add onion, bacon and garlic, cook, stirring, until bacon is crisp. Stir in mushrooms, olives, paste and thyme; cool.
Makes 8.

PESTO SWIRLS

3 cups (450g) self-raising flour
1/4 teaspoon salt
90g butter, chopped
2 tablespoons chopped fresh basil
1 1/4 cups (310ml) milk, approximately
2 tablespoons finely grated
parmesan cheese

FILLING
1/2 cup (100g) ricotta cheese
1/2 cup (40g) coarsely grated
parmesan cheese
1/3 cup (80ml) bottled pesto
1/4 cup (40g) pine nuts, toasted
1/4 cup (35g) sun-dried tomatoes in oil,
drained, chopped
1 clove garlic, crushed
1 teaspoon seasoned pepper

Sift flour and salt into large bowl, rub in butter. Add basil, stir in enough milk to mix to a soft, sticky dough. Turn dough onto floured surface, knead until smooth. Roll dough to 25cm x 40cm rectangle, spread with filling. Roll up from long side, like a Swiss roll. Cut roll into 16 slices, place cut-side-up about 3cm apart on greased oven trays. Sprinkle with cheese. Bake in moderately hot oven about 15 minutes.
Filling: Combine all ingredients in bowl.
Makes 16.

ABOVE: Pizza Buns.
RIGHT: Pesto Swirls.

Lebanese cucumber

Glossary

Here are some names, terms and alternatives to help everyone use and understand our recipes perfectly.

ALMONDS:
Blanched: nuts with skins removed.
Flaked: sliced nuts.
Ground: we used packaged commercially ground nuts.
Kernels: whole nuts with skins.
Slivered: nuts cut lengthways.

BACON RASHERS: bacon slices.

BAKING POWDER: a raising agent consisting of a starch, but mostly cream of tartar and bicarbonate of soda in the proportions of 1 level teaspoon of cream of tartar to 1/2 level teaspoon bicarbonate of soda. This is equivalent to 2 teaspoons of baking powder.

BEETROOT: regular round beet.

BICARBONATE OF SODA: baking soda.

BRAN FLAKES: packaged breakfast cereal.

BREADCRUMBS:
Packaged: use fine packaged crumbs.
Stale: use 1- or 2-day-old bread made into crumbs by grating, blending or processing.

BURGHUL (bulghur wheat or bulgar)**:** wheat grains are steamed, dried and crushed; often confused with cracked wheat.

Green shallots

Chives

BUTTER: use salted or unsalted (also called sweet) butter; 125g is equal to 1 stick of butter.

BUTTERNUT COOKIES: packaged biscuits made from sugar, flour, rolled oats, butter, coconut and golden syrup.

CHEESE:
Blue vein: we used a soft blue vein cheese.
Feta: a soft Greek cheese with a sharp, salty taste.
Gruyere: a Swiss cheese with small holes and a nutty flavour.
Hard goats': made from goats' milk.
Packaged cream: also known as Philly.
Parmesan: sharp-tasting hard cheese.
Ricotta: fresh, unripened, light curd cheese.
Smoked: use a firm smoked cheese.
Tasty cheddar: mature-tasting, firm-textured cheese.

CHICK PEAS: garbanzos.

CHOCOLATE:
Dark: we used a good-quality cooking chocolate.
Choc Bits: morsels of dark chocolate; they do not melt during baking.
Orange thins: thin chocolates with orange-flavoured filling; any thin pieces of chocolate can be used.
White Bits: morsels of white chocolate; they do not melt during baking.

CHORIZO: spicy pork sausage.

COCONUT: use desiccated coconut, unless otherwise specified.
Cream: available in cans and cartons.
Flaked: flaked dried coconut flesh.
Milk: available in cans.
Shredded: thin strips of dried coconut.

CORNMEAL: ground dried corn (maize); similar to polenta but pale yellow and finer. One can be substituted for the other, but textures will vary.

CRACKED BUCKWHEAT (kasha)**:** crushed buckwheat seeds.

CREAM: fresh pouring cream; has a minimum fat content of 35 percent.
Sour: a thick, commercially cultured soured cream containing not less than 35 per cent fat.
Thickened (whipping): has a minimum fat content of 35 per cent and contains a thickener.

CURRY POWDER: a convenient combination of powdered spices consisting of chilli, coriander, cumin, fennel, fenugreek and turmeric in varying proportions.

CUSTARD POWDER: vanilla pudding mix.

ENGLISH SPINACH: a soft-leaved vegetable, more delicate in taste than silverbeet; young silverbeet can be substituted.

ESSENCE: extract.

FLOUR:
Plain: all-purpose.
Rye: milled from rye grains.
Self-raising: substitute plain (all-purpose) flour and baking powder in the proportions of 1 cup (150g) plain flour to 2 level teaspoons baking powder. Sift together several times before using.
Wholemeal plain: wholewheat flour without the addition of baking powder.
Wholemeal self-raising: wholewheat self-raising flour; add baking powder to wholemeal plain flour as above to make wholemeal self-raising flour.

GHEE: a pure butter fat, ghee can be heated to higher temperatures than butter without burning because of the lack of salts and milk solids.

GOLDEN SYRUP: also known as light treacle; is a sweetener made from evaporated sugar cane juice; maple or pancake syrup or honey can be substituted, but the flavour will vary.

GRAND MARNIER: orange-flavoured liqueur.

JAM: conserve.

Kumara

Desiccated coconut

Coconut milk

Coconut cream

Shredded coconut

Flaked coconut

COCONUT

JERSEY CARAMELS: confectionery made from sugar, glucose, condensed milk, flour, oil and gelatine.

KIBBLED RYE: cracked rye grains.

KUMARA: orange sweet potato.

LEBANESE CUCUMBER: thin-skinned variety also known as European or burpless cucumber.

MACADAMIAS: Queensland or Hawaiian nuts.

MAPLE-FLAVOURED SYRUP: golden or pancake syrup or honey can be substituted, but the flavour will vary.

MARSALA: a sweet, fortified wine.

MARS BAR: confectionery bar consisting of creamy caramel and soft nougat encased in milk chocolate.

MILK: we used full-cream homogenised milk unless otherwise specified.

Buttermilk: made by adding a culture to skim milk to give a slightly acidic flavour; a low-fat milk can be substituted.

Sweetened condensed: we used canned milk with 60 per cent of the water removed, and remaining milk sweetened with sugar.

MIXED DRIED FRUIT: a combination of sultanas, raisins, currants, mixed peel and cherries.

MIXED PEEL: candied citrus peel.

MIXED SPICE: a blend of ground spices usually consisting of cinnamon, allspice (pimento) and nutmeg.

MOLASSES: the thick, syrupy end product of raw sugar manufacturing or refining.

MUSTARD:
Dijon: a hot French mustard.
Dry: powdered mustard seeds.
Seeded: a French-style textured mustard with crushed mustard seeds.

NUTELLA: chocolate hazelnut spread.

OAT BRAN: the outer layer of oat grains.

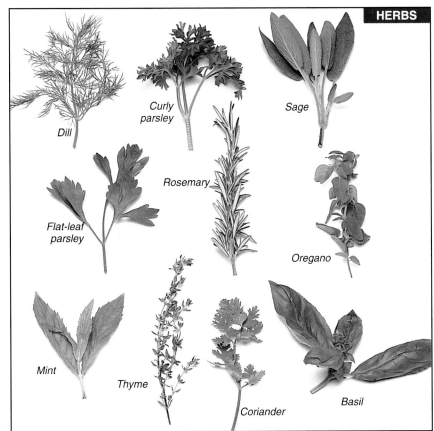

HERBS

Dill

Curly parsley

Sage

Flat-leaf parsley

Rosemary

Oregano

Mint

Thyme

Coriander

Basil

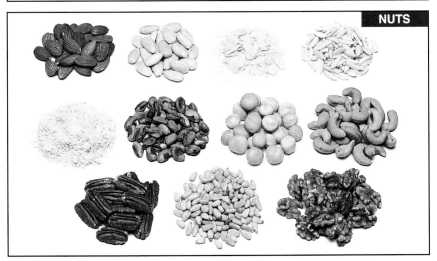

NUTS

Back row: Almond kernels; Blanched almonds; Flaked almonds; Slivered almonds
Middle row: Ground almonds; Pistachios; Macadamias; Unsalted roasted cashews
Front row: Pecans; Pine nuts; Walnuts

SUGAR

*Top row: White sugar; Brown sugar; Caster sugar
Second row: Demerara sugar; Icing sugar
mixture; Raw sugar*

SEEDS

*Top row: Caraway seeds; Coriander seeds; Cumin seeds
Middle row: Linseeds; Poppyseeds; Sesame seeds
Front row: Sunflower seed kernels; Pumpkin seed kernels (pepitas)*

OIL:
Light olive: a mild-flavoured olive oil.
Olive: a blend of refined and virgin olive oils, good for everyday cooking.
Vegetable: we used a polyunsaturated vegetable oil.

PAPRIKA: ground dried peppers; flavour varies from mild and sweet to considerably hotter, depending on the variety of pepper.

PASTRAMI: spicy smoked beef, ready to eat when bought.

PEPPER:
Black: black peppercorns are the ripened fruit of a perennial vine. We used both cracked and ground black pepper.
Cayenne: also known as chilli pepper.
Seasoned: a combination of black pepper, sugar and bell pepper.

PEPPERS: capsicum or bell peppers.

PINE NUTS: small, cream-coloured soft kernels.

Rhubarb

PRUNES: whole dried plums.
PUMPKIN: vegetable with golden flesh; any type of pumpkin can be used.
RHUBARB: a vegetable with pinkish stalks that are generally cooked and eaten as a fruit.
RIND: zest.
RUM, DARK: we used an underproof (not overproof) rum.
SAMBAL OELEK: also ulek or olek; a salty paste made from ground chillies.
SEMOLINA: coarsely milled inner part of wheat grains.
STOCK POWDER: we used chicken and vegetable stock powders; 1 teaspoon of stock powder is equal to 1 small stock cube.
SUGAR: we used coarse granulated table sugar, also known as crystal sugar, unless otherwise specified.
Brown: a soft, fine granulated sugar containing molasses.
Caster: also known as superfine, it is a fine granulated table sugar.
Demerara: golden crystal sugar.
Icing: also known as confectioners' sugar or powdered sugar. Icing sugar mixture contains cornflour; use pure icing sugar, if specified.
Raw: natural brown granulated sugar.

SULTANAS: golden raisins.
YEAST: allow 2 teaspoons (7g) dry yeast to each 15g compressed yeast if substituting one for the other; also see page 44 of this book for helpful information.
ZUCCHINI: courgette.

English spinach

Burghul

Cracked buckwheat

Cornmeal

Kibbled rye

Index

THE EASY AUSSIE BREAD MAKER

You can soon take the hard work out of kneading dough with a new, simple-to-use mixer and kneader called the Easy Knead Aussie Doughmaker. Stand it on a flat surface, place the ingredients in the bowl, turn the handle, and in minutes the dough is ready for proving then baking.

The invention of Bruce Doreian and his son Graeme, of Dromana, Victoria, the doughmaker is constructed from high-impact, food-grade plastic, and can process from 250g to 700g of dry ingredients at a time.

It comes with instructions and a year's guarantee.

You can buy the doughmaker alone, or as part of a kit called Aussie Bakery, which also includes a prover box, measuring container, 450g black tin with release coating, and a mini loaf tin. Easy Knead organic all-natural bread mixes are also available.

For details and prices, write to Easy Knead Breadmaking, PO Box 383, Dromana, Victoria, 3936; telephone (059) 81 4109; fax (059) 81 2799.

QUICK CONVERSION GUIDE

Wherever you live in the world you can use our recipes with the help of our easy-to-follow conversions for all your cooking needs. These conversions are approximate only. The difference between the exact and approximate conversions of liquid and dry measures amounts to only a teaspoon or two, and will not make any difference to your cooking results.

MEASURING EQUIPMENT

The difference between measuring cups internationally is minimal within 2 or 3 teaspoons' difference. (For the record, 1 Australian metric measuring cup will hold approximately 250ml.) The most accurate way of measuring dry ingredients is to weigh them. When measuring liquids use a clear glass or plastic jug with metric markings.

If you would like the measuring cups and spoons as used in our Test Kitchen, turn to page 128 for details and order coupon. In this book we use metric measuring cups and spoons approved by Standards Australia.

● a graduated set of four cups for measuring dry ingredients; the sizes are marked on the cups.
● a graduated set of four spoons for measuring dry and liquid ingredients; the amounts are marked on the spoons.
● 1 TEASPOON: 5ml.
● 1 TABLESPOON: 20ml.

NOTE: NZ, CANADA, USA AND UK ALL USE 15ml TABLESPOONS.
ALL CUP AND SPOON MEASUREMENTS ARE LEVEL.

DRY MEASURES

METRIC	IMPERIAL
15g	½oz
30g	1oz
60g	2oz
90g	3oz
125g	4oz (¼lb)
155g	5oz
185g	6oz
220g	7oz
250g	8oz (½lb)
280g	9oz
315g	10oz
345g	11oz
375g	12oz (¾lb)
410g	13oz
440g	14oz
470g	15oz
500g	16oz (1lb)
750g	24oz (1½lb)
1kg	32oz (2lb)

LIQUID MEASURES

METRIC	IMPERIAL
30ml	1 fluid oz
60ml	2 fluid oz
100ml	3 fluid oz
125ml	4 fluid oz
150ml	5 fluid oz (¼ pint/1 gill)
190ml	6 fluid oz
250ml	8 fluid oz
300ml	10 fluid oz (½ pint)
500ml	16 fluid oz
600ml	20 fluid oz (1 pint)
1000ml (1 litre)	1¾ pints

WE USE LARGE EGGS WITH AN AVERAGE WEIGHT OF 60g

HELPFUL MEASURES

METRIC	IMPERIAL
3mm	⅛in
6mm	¼in
1cm	½in
2cm	¾in
2.5cm	1in
5cm	2in
6cm	2½in
8cm	3in
10cm	4in
13cm	5in
15cm	6in
18cm	7in
20cm	8in
23cm	9in
25cm	10in
28cm	11in
30cm	12in (1ft)

HOW TO MEASURE

When using the graduated metric measuring cups, it is important to shake the dry ingredients loosely into the required cup. Do not tap the cup on the bench, or pack the ingredients into the cup unless otherwise directed. Level top of cup with knife. When using graduated metric measuring spoons, level top of spoon with knife. When measuring liquids in the jug, place jug on flat surface, check for accuracy at eye level.

OVEN TEMPERATURES

These oven temperatures are only a guide; we've given you the lower degree of heat. Always check the manufacturer's manual.

	C° (Celsius)	F° (Fahrenheit)	Gas Mark
Very slow	120	250	1
Slow	150	300	2
Moderately slow	160	325	3
Moderate	180 – 190	350 – 375	4
Moderately hot	200 – 210	400 – 425	5
Hot	220 – 230	450 – 475	6
Very hot	240 – 250	500 – 525	7

TWO GREAT OFFERS FROM THE AWW HOME LIBRARY

Here's the perfect way to keep your Home Library books in order, clean and within easy reach. More than a dozen books fit into this smart silver grey vinyl folder. PRICE: Australia $11.95; elsewhere $21.95; prices include postage and handling. To order your holder, see the details below.

All recipes in the AWW Home Library are created using Australia's unique system of metric cups and spoons. While it is relatively easy for overseas readers to make any minor conversions required, it is easier still to own this durable set of Australian cups and spoons (photographed). PRICE : Australia: $5.95; New Zealand: $A8.00; elsewhere: $A9.95; prices include postage & handling.
his offer is available in all countries.

TO ORDER YOUR METRIC MEASURING SET OR BOOK HOLDER:

PHONE: Have your credit card details ready. Sydney: (02) 260 0035; **elsewhere in Australia:** 008 252 515 (free call, Mon-Fri, 9am-5pm) or FAX your order to (02) 267 4363 or MAIL your order by photocopying or cutting out and completing the coupon below.

PAYMENT: **Australian residents:** We accept the credit cards listed, money orders and cheques. **Overseas residents:** We accept the credit cards listed, drafts in $A drawn on an Australian bank, also English, New Zealand and U.S. cheques in the currency of the country of issue.
Credit card charges are at the exchange rate current at the time of payment.

Please photocopy and complete coupon and fax or send to:
AWW Home Library Reader Offer, ACP Direct, PO Box 7036, Sydney 2001.

❏ Metric Measuring Set   ❏ Holder

Please indicate number(s) required.

Mr/Mrs/Ms _____

Address _____

_____

Postcode _____ Country_____

Ph: ( ) _____Bus. Hour: _____

I enclose my cheque/money order for $ _____ payable to ACP Direct

OR: please charge my:

❏ Bankcard ❏ Visa ❏ MasterCard ❏ Diners Club ❏ Amex

□□□□□□□□□□□□□□□□□□□ Exp. Date ___/__

Cardholder's signature _____

(Please allow up to 30 days for delivery within Australia. Allow up to 6 weeks for overseas deliveries.)

Both offers expire 30/6/96.   AWSF96